MW00928465

THE
POWER IN
WAITING

BY:

CARLA CANNON

Copyright © 2013 by Carla Cannon
All rights reserved.

This book or any portion thereof may not be reproduced or
used in any manner whatsoever without the express written
permission of the publisher except for the use of brief
quotations in a book review.

Printed in the United States of America

First Printing, 2013

ISBN 978-1482668445

Ordering Information:

Quantity Sales. Special discounts are available on quantity
purchases by corporations, associations, and others. For
details, contact Carla Cannon at
Carla@WomenOfStandard.org or call 252-717-5583.

DEDICATION

I dedicate this book to my daughter, Patience Armoni Harris, whom I like to call *Princess Patience*. You add so much joy to Mommy's life and there are no words that can express how much you mean to me. Mommy broke free for you. Remember that God will never disappoint you. Therefore, no matter how good life gets or how bad things may seem, always turn to Him. You are never alone, for He is always with you. I love you my angel.

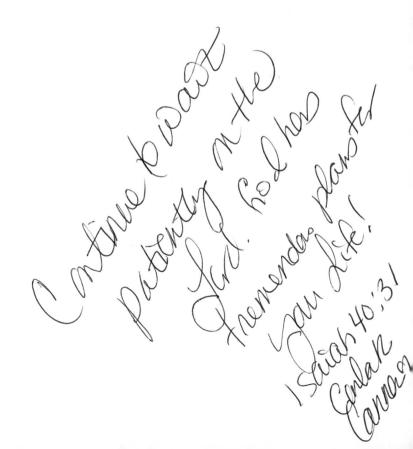

ACKNOWLEDGEMENTS

To the most important woman in my life, my mother, Felicia C. Hagans: thank you for never giving up on me. You are truly one of the reasons why I am still here today. You never left my side. You never gave up on me or threw me away when my world appeared dark. During my transition you never disowned me, but you always loved me and even showed tough love at times that I had to learn to appreciate. I dedicate this book to you as well Mom because believe it or not at times, you carried me when I could not find enough strength within myself to walk on my own. Guess what else? One day very soon, you will get that check I have always promised you of $10,000. Watch and see! I love you and again, thank you!

To my father, Roscoe Cannon: You are a very special man in my life although we have had various ups and downs. My heart still longs for you and I have a space that only you can fill. I love you Dad!

To my big sister, Latisha Lashae' Coward: I have always wanted to be like you. I wanted to dance like you, do hair like you, jump double-dutch like you, and even dress like you! But today, I must admit that I am finally satisfied with the woman I have become and am yet still evolving into. Thank you for loving me and for always being there when I needed you. Although you never said too much when I would call you crying, you being there to listen and sometimes make me laugh were enough for me. I pray your little sister has made you proud! I love you sis!

To my baby sister, Rhonda Lachelle Harper: know that you are a winner. You are somebody special and God made you just as He designed you to be! Your past is over; therefore no longer look back, but press forward, for there are great things in store for you! Believe in yourself and never allow what others say to cause you to think negatively about who God has created you to be! You are a woman of standard and you are also destined to worship! Thank you for always being here by my side. It means more than you'll ever know.

To my baby sister, Diana Williams: I love you girlie and although we have been through a lot know that not even blood can separate us for we are sisters for life! I love you and know that you have what it takes to be all God has created you to be! I hold you dear to my heart and I pray our relationship is fully restored.

To my maternal Grandmother, Lillie Ruth Coward, who died when I was a toddler and I vaguely remember: Grandma, my mom always told me the story of how you tried to potty train me for the longest and the day that you died, my mom states I never wet the bed again. Grandma, I always imagined what it would have been like to have you in my life. To hear you say, *"I love you"* or to snap pictures of you hugging your great-granddaughter, Patience. Although you died when I was young, I carry you in my heart and I look at your pictures often and think of what life would be like if you were still here. I love you Grandma, and I beg to differ that it is possible to miss something you never had.

To my paternal Grandmother, Rachel Cannon, who passed away when I was younger as well: Grandma, I remember going with you from door to door witnessing to God's people. I remember the lyrics to your favorite song, *"Life Without End At Last."* I never really knew the rhythm of that song; however, I do recall my dad telling me it was one of your favorites. So, I would make up my own beat and sing it just to feel closer to you. I wish you could see all that your granddaughter has become. I love you Grandma, and miss you so much.

To a special friend, Roosevelt Ethridge, Jr.: thank you for always believing in me and interceding on my behalf during the toughest times of my life.

To my mentor, Nanette Floyd Patterson, *The Vision Manifestation Queen* of Knightdale, NC: thank you so much for investing in my future. Thank you for loving me and for seeing enough God in me to speak life into me. I give you my heartfelt thanks for providing me with tools to help me overcome my current mindset to manifest the vision that God has for my life. I thank you so much for everything; you are indeed the Vision Manifestation Queen! I love you!

To my new leaders, Pastor Wil & First Lady, Dr. Grace Nichols (Victorious Praise Fellowship C.O.G.I.C. Durham, NC): you two are truly my spiritual mother and father. I have always dreamed of having leaders like you. Pastor Wil, thank you for loving First Lady the way you do and for showing me how a man is to love his wife. Dr. Grace, you are what I call the epitome of a Proverbs 31 woman and a true woman of standard indeed. Thank you for being a woman of excellence and teaching the younger generation how to be the women that God has chosen and created us to be. Thank you also for the push to finish this book and for simply being available and giving so much of yourselves to ministry. This was truly a divine connection. Love you both!

To my spiritual mom, Minister Liz Johnson: Words can't express what you mean to me. Thank you for interceding for me and encouraging me to press forward when many were trying to hold me back. Thank you for not turning your back on me when many did. It is because of people like you that I refuse to give up. How can you give up when you have *real* prayer warriors on your side? I am so blessed to have you in my life.

To a lady who is like another mom to me, Mrs. Lita Ward. I never knew when we met years ago the Lord would bring us together the way He has. Thank you for showing me what true agape love is all about. I often call you *"My Lita"* because I truly believe the Lord sent you to be a part of my destiny. I love you!

Bishop T.L. Penny of Shubach Ministries in Sumter, SC: I remember the first time God used you to speak over my life. After that, I was forever changed. I watched the words you spoke become evident in my life within a six-month timeframe. Thank you for being a positive example for young women in the Lord, such as myself. I love you! A special thank you also to Elder Beverly Richbow: I love you lady for it was through you that I was able to meet Bishop Penny. Thank you for speaking on my behalf.

To my big brother, Craig Damon (and wife Sherry Sanders), I am still amazed at the people the Lord has placed within my circle. Thank you for speaking life when so many people were speaking death. When I call you and say, *"Bro, I need you,"* you never ask what's wrong. You just go straight into big brother mode and begin to uplift me, and you are always on point. You were one of the people God used to help me keep standing when it got tough and I wanted to quit. So, I say thank you! Kiss Sherry and the kids for me! Love you!

To Pastor Vanessa Byrd of Paradise Outreach Ministries, Greenville, NC: I want to thank you for sending words of comfort and helping me understand this season the Lord has me in. I am in my defining moment and I bless God for connecting me with people such as you. I love you!

Joyce Meyer: Although, I have never met you personally, I pray this book reaches your hands. Your ministry helped change my life. It was because of books like, *The Battlefield of the Mind, Never Give Up,* and *Enjoying Where You Are on the Way to Where You Are Going* that changed my life forever! I read *Change Your Words Change Your Life* while in my waiting process and your ministry has been a tremendous blessing. I shall meet you one day and extend to you a hug to express my gratitude of thanks for daring to be different and stepping out when God called you to lead as a woman when it was not popular and very much frowned upon. You are a spiritual mother/mentor to me as well, and I praise God in advance for the day I am blessed to be in your presence, for it shall come to pass!

There are so many people I could thank for praying me through, but I will only name a few: Pastor Darron Carmon (Rebuild Christian Center/Greenville, NC): you will always remain special to me, for God used you to help me walk out my deliverance. I was truly in a life or death situation and it was your wisdom that God imparted into you that helped me to stand. Thank you so much for being available and allowing God to use you. Pastor Dameion Royal (Contending for the Faith Ministries Wilson, NC): I bless God for you! You too were a part of my deliverance process. When I came in your office with my messed up self, you didn't judge me, but you allowed the Lord to use you to help me and for that, I say thank you. Apostle Ella Grimes (Miracle Deliverance Holiness Church, Greenville, NC): you prayed for me from the beginning and I will never forget all the things you taught me. Although we don't talk much now, know that I love you and truly thank you for praying over me and always speaking life. To Nocomus Harris: thank you for giving me the best gift in the world, our daughter Patience Harris. To my cousin Tuwanna Rouse: thank you for loving me and always encouraging me. To my aunt Roberta Coward, thank you for being my number one fan! P.S. I am going to see what I can do about getting you your own show because you are HILARIOUS girl! To my angel and friend, Erica Patrick: thank you girl for always being there when I needed you. When God sends my husband as promised, you will be my matron of honor! Love you! To my special friend Tarinna Terrell, girl I don't know how we became connected but I bless the Lord for the connection. You are indeed a prophet and I know the Lord has assigned you to me in this season.

How special I must be to have my very own prophet. Continue to speak what the Lord tells you to speak and I pray my heart is always open to receiving. I love you and thank you so much! To my big sister in the Gospel, Pastor Ethel James (Oil of Zion International Ministries/Raleigh, NC): thank you for always making time for me and for being authentic. I have seen a lot of people come and go in my life, but I have a feeling it won't be easy getting rid of you. Your little, giant sister (as you call me) loves you! To everyone whose name I did not call, please know that I love and appreciate you. Lastly, to everyone who said I would never amount to anything, who gave up on me, who judged me because of my struggles, I just want to say…THANK YOU! It was you who helped push me into my destiny!

CONTENTS

FOREWORD

I am truly honored to be writing this foreword. As an Ordained Elder, Licensed Professional Counselor, and Master HIScoach, I find so much joy and liberation when someone like Carla is so transparent that they allow God to use their entire design to bless the people of God. In spite of yielding to people who said that some of the topics discussed should be kept private, Carla made a decision to yield to God's call to write this book. This was a call that required her to reveal herself in such a way that social consequences could be costly.

In this book, Carla is as transparent as clear glass, not worrying about being shattered. Carla becomes transparent about her life, personal experience of being labeled, and her deliverance from homosexuality amongst other things contrary to God. She truly shares that deliverance is available to us all. This book is part of her waiting. The Word of God says that you will know a person by the fruit they produce. This book is just one piece of fruit that God has commissioned her to produce. This fruit is ripe, sweet, and good. As you read this ordained masterpiece, you will begin to believe that the weight of waiting is part of the overall plan. I firmly believe that God uses a person's testimony to deliver others. Individuals who read this book will gain self-permission to allow themselves to truly experience the "waiting" period. Experiencing the "waiting" period allows you to produce the fruit that God predestinated to manifest.

8

But they that wait upon the Lord shall renew their strength; they shall mount up with wings as eagles; they shall run, and not be weary; and they shall walk, and not faint. - Isaiah 40:31 - (KJV)

At some point during the "waiting," Carla understood that God would deliver her for a good purpose. And this purpose is now!

The LORD said, "Surely I will deliver you for a good purpose; surely I will make your enemies plead with you in times of disaster and times of distress. Jeremiah 15:11 (NIV)

I encourage all who read this book to strive to understand the "waiting" period of their life, and make a decision to allow God to use them in a BIG way!

Nanette Floyd Patterson, MA, LPC, Master HIScoach
"The Vision Manifestation Queen"

Introduction

Like many of you, I too have heard prophecy after prophecy regarding all the marvelous things the Lord was *going* to do in my life; yet things always seemed to get much worse before they got better. I am still amazed at how the Lord has me writing a book to encourage you when at this point in my life I feel I am in need of major encouragement. In the time that this book was written, I was in a season where I had absolutely no clue what the Lord was doing in my life. I can't begin to count how many times I was told that money would never be an option for me, but yet I struggled to pay my bills every month. I can't begin to tell you how many times I was prophesied to that the Lord was going to bless me with the house I was *supposed* to be living in, only to get a phone call from the property management company informing me that the landlord wanted her home back and I had one month to find somewhere else to live. I had recently moved into the place only a few months prior and absolutely loved it! Honestly, I thought that was the house the preacher had mentioned, but boy was I wrong! My daughter and I ended up having to move into a much smaller home that I hated because I had to sell some of my furniture because my previous home was much larger. I had to make this new, smaller place called "home" work. I needed to explain all of that to tell you that sometimes what we ask God for is entirely too small for what He actually wants to bless us with. The Word of God tells us that the earth is the Lord's and the fullness thereof. If that is the case, why do we constantly believe God can do it for everyone else except for us? We help pray others to their next level. We pray them out of bondage. We pray they get the job or the new promotion, or that their son or daughter gets saved. But when it comes to us and our individual lives, we second guess if God can and will really do it for us. I stand to ask you this question on today: Why not you? Why don't you believe God can do it for you? Is it because of your bloodline? Is it because of your past? Is it because of what you did last night? Brother or sister, I am here to tell you that if you have repented and truly turned away from the sin of your yesterday, then old things have passed away and behold, all things have become new (*2 Corinthians 5:17*).

You are reading the book of a woman with no college education, one who barely graduated from high school, who grew up feeling like a reject and a failure because she became pregnant at the age of sixteen. If that's not bad enough, due to the rejection and pain she experienced, she began to seek love in all the wrong places. She ended up in one bad relationship after another with men and was later introduced to homosexuality, in which she dwelled in for five long years. Now you may say, five years is not a long time, but I beg to differ. Indeed it is when you are raising a child, and you don't even know whether you are coming or going. I shared a part of my testimony with you to show you that people don't determine who God uses. But God chooses whom He may and I have noticed Him raising up those who have been cast away. He is clearing the stage from all those who appear to have it all together, but have bodies in their closets, not skeletons, as Bishop T. L. Penny would say it. God is replacing them with those of us who are pure, holy

11

and willing to lay it all on the line for Jesus and live according to His Word!

Many are out here preaching God's Word, but a large portion of them live contrary lives to the words they preach every Sunday. As my Pastor Wil Nichols would say, because of this, I have developed godly anger when I see others prosper when I know they are leading people astray or living contrary lives compared to the ones they profess. I develop godly anger when I see others mistreated when they stand for righteousness' sake and the very folk that are to be with them, choose not to stand up for them and literally throw them to the wolves. Well, the times are changing and although it may not feel like it or look like it, God is working things out on your behalf! I'm here to let you know that your time is coming, but you must be willing to undergo the process and allow God to deal with you where you are first in order to prepare you for the greatness that lies ahead! We must believe and have faith in the God that we serve.

One thing I have noticed, especially in the body of Christ, is out of all of the other religions, we as Christians don't even believe the Bible that we often quote. When God says you are the head and not the tail, the lender and not the borrower, above and not beneath, a royal priesthood, He means just that (*Deuteronomy 28:13; Proverbs 22:7; 1 Peter 2:9*). In order for us to live life more abundantly, we must learn to take God at His Word and believe that He is. One thing that Pastor Sheryl Brady said that has always stuck with me is this: "*We must believe that God is whatever we need Him to be, whenever we need Him to be it."*

So today, whatever the promise is that you are waiting for the Lord to fulfill, know that you are being strengthened while you wait. You are being restored and you are being replenished. You must know that you know, that you know, that you know that your God is going to do everything He said He would do according to His Word! It is not enough to just know; you must be confident that the work He has begun, He is going to complete (**Philippians 1:6**). We must know that He only promised to fulfill His Word. So, how can we know what His promises are if we don't dig into His Word and find them? For that reason, here and now, I challenge you to grab your journal, along with your Bible, and get into your secret, quiet place and allow the Lord to speak to you as I talk with you briefly about...THE....POWER....IN...WAITING!

Foundational scripture for this book:

Isaiah 40:31: But they that wait upon the Lord shall renew their strength, they shall mount up with wings as eagles; they shall run and not be weary; and they shall walk and not faint.

CHAPTER 1: UNDERSTANDING PROPHECY

By First Understanding My Story

I pray that you do not begin this book thinking I have a lot of deep things to say; I would hate to disappoint you. I believe in keeping things concise and to the point. I am truly listening to the voice of God as I write this unto you. When it comes to understanding prophecy, I am reminded of the scripture, Jeremiah 29:11, *"For I know the thoughts that I think toward you," says the Lord, "thoughts of peace and not of evil, to give you an expected end."* Along with that, I am reminded of Romans 8:28, *"And we know that all things work together for good to them that love God, to those who are the called according to His purpose."* Now, I'm sure you are thinking these scriptures do not coincide or are in agreement. But I will prove that they are!

Jeremiah 29:11 reveals to us the thoughts God has for us, which means we are on the mind of God. I want you to pause for a moment and think of just how awesome that really is. In spite of feeling that your existence may not matter or that no one cares, allow this to comfort you in knowing that you are on the mind of God and He is going to allow everything you have ever gone through or experienced to work for your good! I just made myself excited! So often, people have a way of making you feel insignificant because you may not drive what they drive, or live in a big house on a hill, which, in their eyes, disqualifies you from being in a certain clique or group!

But I am reminded of God's Word that says being a friend of the world is an enemy of God (*James 4:4*).

We have to learn how to dissect scriptures versus memorizing them, solely to gain a better understanding of God's Word, as well as to properly interpret it. I firmly believe that memorization without application leads to the ultimate feelings of emptiness and a life lacking substance. If we remember the Word of God, but do not apply it to our lives, we are then held responsible for the Word we have heard. Did you know that? Many of us sit in bible study after bible study, and go right back out, doing the very things our pastors and leaders have taught us *not* to do according to the Word of God. The book of Romans goes on to say that *all* things, not some things, not many things, but *all* things will work together for our good. Like you, I have been through a lot of things during my few years here on this earth. I know what it feels like to be betrayed; I also know what it feels like to betray someone else. I know what it feels like to be cheated on and I also know what it feels like to be the cheater. I know what it feels like to be lied to and I also know what it feels like to be a liar. The point I'm trying to make is no matter who did what to me, or what I did to them, it did not remove the hand of God off of my life. That's an empowering word for somebody right there!

Some of you have been lied to or tricked into believing that you have messed up so badly and now because of it, God can't use you! The devil is a liar and it is the furthest thing from the truth. This is why it is so important to get into the Word of God, where you can receive encouragement, wisdom and the revelatory mysteries of God first-hand.

David was a murderer and an adulterer, but he was also someone who was close to God's heart. Paul was a murderer of Christians who was eventually converted and became one of Jesus' right-hand men and a great apostle! It really does not matter where you have been or what you have done; when true repentance takes place, even the sky is no limit as it pertains to what the Lord can and will do for you! When I think back over all of the mistakes I have made, I realize that all of my bad choices have only pushed me closer to God. I know you may be wondering how that is possible, so let me explain. When I was betrayed, it made me get on my face and seek the Lord because I was wounded and didn't understand what I had done to deserve to be treated in that manner. But in spite of what happened to me, I always remembered to pray. It is true that many of us, during our childhood, were taught to do what was and is right to do; yet we strayed away from it. However, the Word of God tells me that God is married to the backslider (*Jeremiah 3:14*). There really is no possible way for me to mess up so badly where God will say, *"Okay, I'm done with you. I take my promises back."* God would never say, *"Carla, I had such great plans for your life, but since you can't seem to get it right, I changed my mind and I will give them to your sister instead."*

Now listen very closely, and don't confuse what I am saying. There is a time if we are walking in rebellion that God will remove His hand from our life, especially if we are not truly sincere in our repentance and we choose to continue in our sin. One thing about the Lord is that He gives us free will and He is the perfect gentleman. He will never force Himself on anyone. We have a choice. Either we can accept Him into our heart as our Lord and personal Savior, or we can reject Him.

Looking back over my life, as I mentioned in my introduction, the Lord delivered me from homosexuality. I know, go ahead and close your mouth because I know it dropped wide open when you saw the word "homosexuality," for that is a topic that many tend to shy away from today. However, it is the very thing the Lord has used in my life as evidence that He is real. During my struggle, I can remember thinking that I would never become free and that I was too far gone from the touch of a man. My body no longer responded to men and women seemed to be what my body desired. I recall one relationship in particular and it was my last relationship with a female. I really had grown tired of living the lifestyle, especially since I was raising a little girl who was watching everything that I did. Now take note, my outer appearance never changed. I was still the same pretty Carla with the beautiful dimples that everyone knew, but my sexual preference and desires had changed.

Consequently, that's one misconception; every person struggling with something may not always *look* like they have a struggle at all. Oh, how I fooled many! I was attending church service after church service, and no one had any discernment to distinguish that although I was attending church regularly, my heart was so far from the Lord. Or, I could say that no one was bold enough to approach me. I recall times when I attended bible study and Sunday morning services weekly with my girlfriend and her family, shouting and crying through almost every service for an entire year. I really wanted to be free, but had no idea what the first steps were to becoming free. Therefore, even though I listened to the preached Word of God and experienced the power of God during the services, I would cry and lay out on the floor, only to go back home and entertain the very things the Lord was trying to deliver me from.

After attending church with my girlfriend and her family for an entire year, I finally told God, *"Okay; for real I need your help! I can't do this alone."* I began to sincerely cry out for help, but I took it one step further. I made an appointment to speak with my pastor to receive counsel on how to free myself from this mess I had made. Let's pause here for a second. Many of us tend to suffer in silence because we grew up with the saying, *"What happens in this house, stays in this house."* There are others who are very private individuals and have the mindset of, *"I don't want everyone in my business."* But the truth is we are designed to need the prayers, assistance and counsel of others. Throughout scripture, we see the Lord teaching us how to treat one another, to be peacemakers, and to love one another. I believe this is so because He never designed us to be able to make it alone. Everybody needs somebody.

I remember watching the movie, *Poetic Justice,* featuring Janet Jackson and deceased rapper, Tupac Shakur. At the beginning of the movie, she said, *"Nobody can make it out of here alone."* The very same principle applies to us as believers. Often when the enemy is fighting and attacking us, we tend to stay in our situations much longer because we are afraid to be transparent with our leaders, our friends, and sometimes family members that we know will help us. Yet, we are steadily beaten upon by the enemy, as our strength is drained from the excessive warfare taking place that we were never designed to fight on our own. Sadly, we remain there for days, weeks, months, even years. See, my excuse for not going to someone sooner was that I allowed the enemy to make me believe no one would understand and that I was stuck. Well, in spite of all of those thoughts, one day I had enough. It was as if I literally saw my life flash before my eyes and I went to my pastor and spilled all the beans.

I didn't hold anything back and he had no idea that it was going on. See, there is a misconception about pastors because they are sent by God. We often expect them to know everything, but the truth is they are human just like you and I. Unless the Lord reveals it, they won't know it, especially if the church consists of a very large congregation.

After receiving counsel from my pastor, I began to pray to the Lord on how I was going to get out of the relationship. I was currently working a full-time job and felt that if I found a second job, that would tie up the majority of my time, along with my daughter, and I wouldn't be able to spend much time with her. I know you may be thinking, *"Well, why didn't you just break up with her?"* That is a very good question, but contrary to what many like to think as it relates to homosexuals, they love just as hard as heterosexuals. When a heterosexual couple is in love, it is no different from homosexual couples. Feelings are feelings, and love is love. Please do not misconstrue what I am saying; I am not condoning this type of relationship, but I am only using my story, my own testimony, to help deliver the message of understanding prophecy that I believe the Lord is leading me to share with you.

Surprisingly, God allowed me to get the second job and I began to work more hours. Gradually, I saw her less and less and eventually, God gave me strength to break up with her. But, here is where many mess up. The power wasn't in my breaking up with her, but the power was in my act of submission, allowing God to break the spirit of homosexuality, lust (and many more that came attached to it) off my life. Truthfully, she was not the first female I had broken up with, saying, *"I can't do this anymore,"* only to do well for a while and then end up in another homosexual relationship a year later. When we are going through changes in our lives or battling things, it is vital that we allow the Lord to fully process us before we try to step out and do what we believe He has called us to do. We will talk about embracing the process in the next chapter, but I wanted to share this point with you before we moved on. Although I ended up in various homosexual relationships, and struggled tremendously in my flesh, God never changed His mind concerning the call He had on my life.

One thing about prophecy is that God shall fulfill it when it is according to His plan and purpose for your life. Let's first understand what the word *prophecy* means.

Webster's Dictionary defines the word *prophecy* as: *an inspired utterance of a prophet; a prediction of something to come.* Now don't get prophecy confused with the word, *prophesy.* Webster defines the word *prophesy* as: *to utter by or as if by divine inspiration; to predict with assurance or on the basis of mystic knowledge.* Now that you understand the difference between the two, let me share this with you. Did you know that you have the power to prophesy over your own life? You don't have to wait on the preacher, your pastor, or mother so and so to lay hands on you because you have the power to lay hands on your own head and call forth whatever the Word of God says is rightfully yours. I believe so often that many of us underestimate ourselves and the power we possess through Jesus. I can recall a lady giving me a Word from the Lord and each time she would do it, she would always begin by saying, *"I'm no preacher, but I hear God saying..."* One day I finally told her, *"Stop discrediting yourself; titles mean nothing. If you hear the Lord, speak what He says and stop speaking when He stops."* To hear from the Lord, all one needs is an ear to hear. If God can speak to a donkey, then surely He can use who He may to deliver His Word. Many of us miss God because we focus on the messenger instead of the message.

When seeking to understand prophecy, it is essential to recognize that whatever God speaks over your life, without a doubt, it shall come to pass. Like we used to say back in the day, *"You can take that to the bank!"* I am reminded of Philippians 1:6 that tells us that the work the Lord has begun in us, He is able to complete it until the day of Jesus Christ. Who is to say that all you had to deal with

21

in your past is not a part of God's blueprint for your destiny? Who is to say that the rape, the abortion, your husband walking out on you, or your wife leaving you for another man, your father or those family members who said you would never amount to anything, were only used as a boomerang to literally thrust you into your destiny?

I can't wait to share with you more knowledge regarding destiny in Chapter 7 entitled, *When Purpose Meets Destiny*. It is extremely significant that we understand that everything we go through is a part of the plan of God for our lives. James reminds us that trials come to increase our patience and to build character, but many of us don't want to go through anything to obtain the promise. We live in a microwave society, where we want to receive a prophecy today and if God doesn't perform it in the next few weeks, we lose our faith and suddenly grow weary in well doing. I remember when my sister began to work out and after a few weeks, she grew weary and slacked off and returned to her old eating habits. Once I noticed this, I asked her why she had stopped her new regimen, and she said it was because each time she checked her weight, the scale numbers did not move! I reminded her that it had only been two weeks and she had to remain determined and believe she could lose the weight. We must learn to be confident in who God has created us to be, or for many of us, who God has transformed us into. Now what about the faith God talks about in His Word? He says that without faith, it is impossible for us to please God. He even bargains with us when He says if you have faith the size of a mustard seed (*Matthew 17:20*), then that is of satisfaction to Him.

But the Lord also gives us an opportunity to grow by telling us that faith comes by hearing and hearing by the Word of God (**Romans 10:17**). Therefore, to gain more faith, what do you believe we should be doing more of? You got it! We should be reading more of the Word of God! While we are in the process of waiting on the Lord to save our children, send us our mate, deliver us out of our situations, we should be professing His Word over our lives until our reality comes to grips with what the Word of God has already said. We must stop speaking out of our feelings and learn to speak only what the Lord says. John 1:1 states, *"In the beginning was the word, and the word was with God and the word was God."* Therefore, that lets me know that God and His Word are one and if I want more of Him, all I have to do is get into His Word. We must learn to stand on God's word and begin to praise Him for the manifestation *before* it actually becomes our natural reality. Like my pastor would say, we must learn to *see* it before we *see* it. Basically, prophecy has no power if you don't believe it. Ouch! I know people will have you to believe that prophecies are spoken and then POOF! They happen just like that! Not true at all! There is something called a waiting period; a process that each of us must undergo before we reach our destiny.

One thing I have learned regarding prophecy is things tend to get worse before they get better. Allow me to use myself for example. I have my own magazine company, *Women of Standard* and *Men of Standard,* which is a monthly publication. It was prophesied to me that God was going to send writers from all over the world to write for my publication. Well, a few weeks after I received this confirmation, two writers from two different parts of the world just up and quit on me. Immediately, I had a decision to make. I could either be moved by what I *see,* or choose to stand on what God *said.* Making the intelligent decision to trust the Lord and stand on His word, He sent three new writers to replace the two that had quit. I'm telling you, God is never slack concerning His promises and nothing ever catches Him by surprise. Rule of thumb: Whenever prophecy is spoken, get ready to be attacked in those exact areas, for it never fails. Many of you reading this today may be struggling financially and you have to go back and revisit the promise. One or two things could be going on: (1) You could be mishandling your finances; or (2) God could be stretching you and teaching you how to trust Him with little as you believe Him for much. Once you gain an understanding of what your purpose is, then you will learn to seek the Lord for the strategy on how to combat the enemy in those particular areas. The enemy is working overtime to keep all of us from reaching our destiny by trying to wear us out in the process. Join me as we enter into Chapter 2 as I prepare you on how to embrace the process God has for your life.

CHAPTER 2: EMBRACING THE PROCESS

This is one problem with the body of Christ. We don't want to be processed. Many are getting saved one day and then calling themselves apostles the next day, without undergoing the process. I know; another ouch! A truth about purpose is we have to understand the significance of the process. The Lord revealed to me that what I went through in my life as it related to struggling with homosexuality and being promiscuous was nothing compared to the significance of the process I had to endure toward being delivered. Although my process was very painful, it also produced much oil. What is oil, you may be asking. Oil represents the anointing of God. I know what it feels like to really love God, but still struggle in your flesh. I know what it feels like to do well for a long time and think you are delivered, only to fall again because of the trauma you experienced from the last incident. Dr. Juanita Bynum said something so profound once. She said, *"Whatever it took for you to break free, you have to do that and then some to stay free!"* I have found this to be so true for not only did I have to fast, pray, and study God's word to become free, but even now, I do that to maintain my deliverance and continue to grow in the things of God. See, many of us are led to Christ, but is there anyone around to help walk us through the process? Your process is not to be taken lightly for it is literally a battle of life and death. Believe it or not, many die (spiritually and/or physically) or lose sight of their purpose or their expected end in the process.

There are many people who have gifts and abilities, Bible lets us know that gifts and callings come without repentance (*Romans 11:29*). But it also tells us to make our callings and elections sure (*2 Peter 1:10*). For example, God has called you to pastor and you move into your calling without undergoing the proper process. At the first sign of trouble, you will be packing up the pews and changing your number to get away from all of the members.

Another thing I believe the Lord wants to teach and remind us of even now is that regardless of the call that is upon our lives, trouble is going to come to test us to see what we are really made of. But we must remember that testing and trials only come to help pull out of us what we never really knew was within us. An unknown author stated, "*You never know what a woman is made of until you put her in hot water.*" That is so true, even today. For example, I used to be a fighter and not that I was the best fighter, I just wasn't afraid to fight you. It didn't matter how big you were; there was never a scared bone in my body. Well, once I got saved and the Lord began to work on me, I never could really tell if I was delivered from fighting or not because God hadn't allowed anyone to approach me in a disrespectful manner. Until one day, a friend of mine got into a fight and I was trying to break up the fight and be the peacemaker. The other girl hit me and before I knew it, I was all over her. I knew then that I needed to get back on the potter's wheel and be made over again because the Word of the Lord clearly advises us to turn the other cheek. Again, this is why the process is vital for it is also a time of learning in which we will gain wisdom from trial and error.

Hopefully, now you can understand why the process is vital. There was something the prolific Bible teacher, Joyce Meyer said that has always stuck with me. She said (paraphrased) our gifts will get us into many places, but due to our lack of character, we are unable to stay there. This is essential for us to learn in our lives today. There are so many get-rich-quick schemes going on that if some of us were to come into a million dollars right now, our lives would immediately go into disarray. Some of us may not return to our jobs on the next day. Because many of us have such a poverty-stricken mindset, instead of investing the money, we would either go out buying houses, cars, and clothes, which all lose value once purchased. Operating in wisdom during this hour is vital to receive all that God has for us. It is during the process that we ask the Lord to equip and prepare us for the great blessings He has for us. The worst thing in the world is to receive a blessing in which you were not prepared for. Why do you think we read of so many "celebrities" dying from drug overdoses or appearing on television shaving off half of their head for no apparent reason? Because not being prepared for success (which includes money) can literally turn someone's world upside down.

Another part of the process is gaining an understanding and receiving clarity of where you are currently. We must know that where we are is not where we will always be. Say this aloud: *"My life now is not how it will be. I will not become complacent, but I will trust God for better. Although it has yet to take place in the natural, God has already released my breakthrough in Heaven and on any given day now, my life can and will change right before my eyes. I will continue to seek and thank the Lord for my deliverance, for my healing, and for all He has promised me."*

I've been in a place where I have no choice but to trust the Lord. One day while I was in worship, I was telling the Lord that I refused to worry another day of my life. I began to tell God aloud that I trust Him and that I take Him at His Word, and I began to call out all of the things that were trying to stress me out. I began to lay them at the feet of Jesus via prayer. I began to anoint my hands and lay hands and pray over all of the bills I had on my counter. I began to tell God how I thank Him for being Jehovah Jireh, my provider. I began to recite his Word, *"My God will supply all my needs according to His riches in glory"* (**Philippians 4:19**). We have to learn to praise God for what has not yet been released as if it has already been manifested in our lives and also trust Him for the shift that is on the way! I hope you caught that! The Word of God encourages us to walk by faith and not by sight and to speak those things that be not as though they were.

For example: Suppose I am a parent and my son is acting crazy, running the streets and getting caught up in the wrong crowds. However, while I carried my son for nine months, the Lord revealed unto me that he would be a prophet and prophesy unto the nations. What I then would have to do is choose to focus on what God *said* instead of what I *see*. I believe this is one of the greatest challenges we tend to face while being human beings living here on earth. This is why during the process, it is of an essence for us to learn who God is. Before we can learn who we are, we must first know who He is, for we were created in His image. Hopefully, this makes sense. The point I am making is that no matter what it looks like during the process, you must know that you are coming out for God's Word already declares it is so. You may ask, "Well Carla, how are you so certain?" Because God's Word declares that He has already overcome the world and we now have His spirit (the Holy Spirit) dwelling on the inside of us. The Word of God also reminds us that greater is He that is within us than He that is within the world. Therefore, nothing can rise up against me that can catch God off guard or be anything that He can't handle. Remember, God is omnipresent (present in all places at all times) and He is omnipotent (all powerful). You know what the other great thing is? We don't even have to fight our battles, for the vengeance is God's, not ours. All we have to do is submit to our process and take everything else to the Lord in prayer.

There are many amazing things that happen during the process: 1.) You learn how to trust in the Lord with your whole heart; 2.) You learn more of Him by getting into His Word because tough times actually push us closer to God. This is why you can't afford to despise your process. 3.) Your identity and purpose is defined. So as you can see, your process actually has benefits. Isn't that amazing? Pause and think about that for a second. The very thing that may be causing pain in your life right now, causing tears to roll down your face, is the very thing that will one day very soon cause you to rejoice. But guess what the secret is? The determining factor of how long we remain in a situation is key as it relates to how we choose to undergo our process and what we do in our times of waiting.

One thing I have learned is that it's not our waiting that matters, but it is *how* we wait. Many of us think we are to sit back quietly and wait *on* God, but the truth is we are to wait *in* God. The difference between waiting on God and waiting in God is this: Waiting *on* God can mean sitting back, twirling your thumbs, waiting for someone to mysteriously or accidently place a million dollars in your bank account. Or waiting on God could be you believing Him for a spouse, but your credit is jacked up, house is nasty and kids are all out of control. What man or woman would want that? Now, pay close attention: Waiting *in* God is just the opposite because those of us who are waiting *in* God are busy working while we wait. While we are trusting God for that million dollars, we are positioning ourselves to receive the wealth we desire. We are reading books on finances and how to budget and track our finances. We are operating in our purpose and doing all we know to do on our end and trusting God to do what we can't. Most millionaires that I know or have read about didn't just wake up one day with a busload of money, but they had to work hard and diligently. They even made a lot of mistakes, but guess what? That's all a part of the what? You got it! It's all a part of the process! So if you are that man or woman trusting God for a spouse, you know that you are to begin preparing for that person to show up in your life. But before they can show up, there must be room for them. Wouldn't it be tragedy for the man or woman of your dreams to show up and you not be prepared for them? During the process, learn all you can and position yourself to obtain all God has for you. Be humble and teachable because another advantage of undergoing the process is your purpose is discovered.

CHAPTER 3: DISCOVERING YOUR PURPOSE

I remember thinking back over my life about all the wrong I had done. All the people I had let down, all the people who had let me down. I began to think of all the people who betrayed me, as well as the ones I betrayed, and how different my life would be had I not gotten pregnant at the age of sixteen. How much further I would be if I had not gotten caught up in an alternative lifestyle for five years and what if I had not played around in college? I would actually have a degree by now. So many thoughts began to run through my mind. I began to also think about my relationship with my biological father and other men that had come and gone out of my life. I tell you, after all of the thinking, I was left depressed. What I came to realize is with one of my personality traits consisting of being a tad bit analytical, I had the problem of thinking myself out of almost anything. We will delve deeper into monitoring your thoughts in Chapter 5, *Don't Let Your Mind Talk You Out of It*. But I literally allowed one thought that came into my mind, turn into another thought, then another thought, and then another. Joyce Meyer often says, *"Think about what you're thinking about."* We really have to monitor where we allow our minds to wander, for where the mind goes, the heart will follow. We must realize that we have the power to overcome in every area of our life. My question to you is: When are you going to tap into that power?

So here I was, not even long ago to be perfectly honest and transparent, with all the great things the Lord was doing in my life. My magazine had recently celebrated its one year anniversary and during our first year, the Lord allowed me to interview some of the world's most prominent people, such as Yolanda Adams, VaShawn Mitchell, Pastor Riva Tims, Dr. Jamal Bryant and more! I don't mean chat with them via email, but I actually conducted phone interviews with them. It was nothing but the favor of God. I had no friends who gave me *the hookup.* All the glory for those opened doors went to nobody but God; for it was Him who allowed each of them to agree to speak with me when they had never heard of *Women of Standard Magazine.* What you have to understand is when the hand of God is upon your life, there is nothing anyone can do to stop it.

About six months ago, the Lord blessed me with a job at one of the top hospitals in the area in which I live. So I packed up all of our belongings and we relocated. Instead of being excited about the transition and thanking God for the *new thing* He was doing in my life, I allowed fear of the unknown to make me sit in my room and cry for days at a time once I had moved. I was no longer near any of my family. I was alone most of the time. I was in a new area in which I didn't know many people. I was completely out of my comfort zone. Honestly, I thought I had made a mistake by relocating. I remember feeling so uncomfortable and wondered what in the world had I done. I no longer had my mom around to help me with my daughter. I no longer had easy access to my daughter's father (whom is a tremendous blessing in her life). I found myself in a major transition. I almost felt like Abraham did when the Lord told him to pack up his things and go to a land in which He would show him.

Well, it had been two weeks and the Lord hadn't *shown* me why He led me to move away. I remember calling my mom crying and her response was not what I expected at all. She said, *"Well, this is what you prayed for so...."* At first, her words stung like a bee, but in an instant, I learned she was right. My prayer to the Lord was that if it was His will for me to relocate, allow me to get the job and for doors to open for me as it related to finding a new home because I had to break my previous lease to relocate. He did just that and more! See, what had to happen was I was in need of a major mind shift. God had brought me to a new place, but I still operated as if I still was where I had previously been. The truth was that my whole life was changing literally right before my eyes. I was reminded that God wanted to do a new thing in my life. He had blessed me with a new job, a new home, a new car, new church family and new friends all within six months. What I didn't know was now I was in the right position and I was well on my way to discovering my purpose in Him.

The transition in my life happened so quickly. I almost can't describe it. I have really seen the hand of God move rather swiftly in my life and the only response I can tell people is that everything changed when I gave God a surrendered "Yes." It wasn't until I told God that nothing else mattered other than pleasing Him. I began to seek His face and say, *"Okay Lord; what do you want me to do?"* It wasn't until I began to spend time in prayer, in God's Word seeking direction that everything began to make sense. I never saw myself being the publisher, better yet the CEO, of my own business. I never saw myself being an author of this very book you are reading. I never saw myself coaching and empowering other women to overcome the pain and failures of their past. But can you guess when it all was manifested? After I went through the *process* and spent time in God's presence. He then began to reveal the purpose for everything I had to endure. He showed me how much power and anointing I had accumulated through all of the pain and tears I had to shed. Like Job, the Lord showed me that He was going to pay me back double for my trouble!

In case you are not familiar with the story of Job, the Bible described Job as an upright man. Job was very wealthy; however, in one day, he lost everything he had, from his children, to his cattle, sheep, possessions; *everything*. His wife tried to persuade him to curse God and die, but Job's reply was, *"Woman you sound foolish!"* Job then cursed the day he was born, for the pain he had to endure was far too much for any one individual to bear. Yet, I am reminded of the scripture that says, *"God won't put anymore on you than what you are able to bear"* (*1 Corinthians 10:13*). Therefore, if God allowed it to happen to Job, it must have meant that Job had what it took to go through it. You may be going through a storm right now that appears to be unbearable and the enemy is trying to convince you that you are not going to make it to the finish line. But the devil is a liar! The Bible declares that you shall walk through the fire and not be burned. You shall run and not be weary, walk and not faint, for God has already

35

given you the power and you are strengthened in Him! Know that you have what it takes to get through this current storm. The Bible also reminds us in Psalm 23 that, *"Yea though I walk through the valley of the shadow of death, I will fear no evil for thy rod and thy staff, they comfort me."* We also know that the Bible tells us that the Lord will never leave us nor forsake us. All of these are promises that we must stand on, no matter what is taking place in the natural.

In a recent trial, I cried out to the Lord, telling Him that I felt He was so far away from me. It was as if God stopped talking. I couldn't feel His presence; therefore, I began to question if I was on the right path. A part of discovering your purpose is having a solid relationship with the Lord. We must know that God is always with us, for He promises to never leave nor forsake us, and we must learn to stand on His word no matter what. I am reminded of the song by Donnie McClurkin, *"I'll Trust You Lord."* In the song, Pastor Donnie is asking us a question, *"What if you can't feel me near you, will you trust me?"* Then he responds by saying, *"Yes I'll trust you."* While sitting at my desk at work listening to Pandora online, songs like that one and *"I'll Trust You"* by James Fortune were playing back to back. I began listening to the words to the songs and realized the Lord was allowing those particular songs to play at that particular time to bring comfort to my spirit. At that moment, I began to tell the Lord, "Thank you." I began to tell Him that although I didn't understand what He was doing in my life, I believed He was working on my behalf. I even told God that I belonged to Him, that I trusted Him, and how much I loved Him.

When was the last time you told God that you love Him? When was the last time you told God, "Thank you"? Better yet, when was the last time you actually praised God right in the midst of all hell breaking loose in your life? An important factor about the process to discovering your purpose is many tears may be shed, many friends may walk away, and you may have to walk alone sometimes. But, it is in those moments when God positions you where it is only you and Him; and that my friend is the best place you should ever want to be. Oftentimes, God will allow the very ones we love the most to hurt us the deepest to help remove some things that God can't elevate us with if we still hold on to it. Does that make sense? God will allow circumstances to define the purpose He has in your life.

Let me tell you what the Lord did for me. God took the very thing that tried to suck the life out of me and He literally transformed it into life itself. Whoa! I know that was deep and God gave me the revelation behind that statement. He told me in these words, *"The enemy literally wanted to take your mind, but I wouldn't let Him. While you were struggling in your flesh, the enemy wanted you to literally go crazy. But I put a shield of protection even around your mind."* After that, I began to hear God say, *"I blocked it."* Let's take a moment and thank the Lord for everything He blocked that tried to take us out before we discovered our purpose in Him!

In my elementary school years, I was diagnosed as having ADHD (Attention Deficit Hyperactivity Disorder) and I remember having to go see a therapist and take all kinds of tests. Then as a young woman, the enemy tried to make me confused in my identity. He convinced me to trade what was natural for the unnatural. The enemy told me that I would never be free and that I was gay and that was how I was going to always be. I admit, for a long time, I actually believed him. But that was until the Holy Ghost stepped in. Some of you have been in your situation so long, and the enemy has convinced you that things will never get better, or that your son will never get out of prison, or that your spouse will never come back home. Perhaps you have a son or daughter who is struggling with their identity, or perhaps it's you who is struggling. Know that I am a living epistle as to what the Lord can do. God can literally do anything except fail. That is not a cute cliché, but that is the story of my life. I don't know about you, but I have a lot of *but God* testimonies. I was trapped and thought I would never break free from Satan's grip, but God! I once tried to take my own life by taking a whole bottle of pills, but God! I once drove 200 feet off the highway in the midst of trees and did not hit any of them, but God! I once didn't know my true value and allowed men to fondle over my body while I lay dormant in search of whom I was, but God!

I know I am not the only one with some *but God* situations. I once found myself struggling to complete tasks because my mind wandered continuously. Now I am sitting here writing this book that you are reading, *but God!* Take a moment and thank the Lord for all of your *but God* situations that you know only He brought you out of!

Please know that you are not stuck. God sees you as the finished product and how beautiful you are unto the

Father. Listen to me; for so long I felt I was identified by my issue. Please know that you are not defined by what you did or who you slept with; for just as God did in the Bible days, He can change your name, too! In the blink of an eye, the Lord can change your life for the better. But you first must believe. If you are still unsure as to what your purpose is in life, I encourage you to think back over all the things you have gone through in life. Normally, our purpose is wrapped in whatever our previous struggles or trials consisted of. God has the power to use the very thing the enemy tried to use to take us out, and God will allow us to profit from it and travel the world, telling the goodness of the Lord!

It is time to discover your purpose! No more just existing! No more second guessing what God has told you! But you need to get busy doing what He has already shown you! Bind up fear, doubt, unbelief, un-forgiveness and move forward. One of the most important things next to giving my life to the Lord was forgiving everyone who hurt me and also forgiving myself. Once for my own therapy, the Lord led me to get a shoe box and tear off small pieces of notebook paper and write down the names of every person that hurt me along with what they did, and those I hurt and what I did, and put it all in the box. I believe I worked on that box for a week. I cried during this process because it was very painful to think back over my past and to release all of the people who had hurt me or said something to me that hurt my feelings. I was still carrying the thought of what they had said to me in my mind years later. God let me know it was time to do this exercise again.I also had to release every person that I had hurt because oftentimes, the enemy will cause us to fall into condemnation when God has forgiven us and cast it all into the sea of forgetfulness. We just have to learn to forgive ourselves and move on. In life, we tend to go through one thing after another, without pausing or stopping to take the time to deal with all the pain and baggage we have accumulated along the way. If we are going to discover our purpose, we first must have a clear mind and release people that are holding us bondage. More importantly, we must forgive ourselves. Some of us have done things that the world would describe as unforgivable, but there is no sin the Lord won't forgive.

David was a man after God's own heart, but David was also the same man who lusted after Bathsheba, plotted to have her husband killed, and then took her to be his wife. Once the Lord began to deal with David, he repented and God forgave Him. Is there something that happened to you, or something you did to someone else, that you are still holding on to? Choose to release it and let it go today! Just let it go! Imagine an eagle trying to fly with one wing. It won't happen. He needs both wings in order to soar! A new author by the name of Tarinna Terrell has published a book entitled, *It's Time to Soar*! I must agree; it is time for us to soar past all the pain, heartache, shame, regret, and guilt, and release it all so the Lord can use all of it for His glory! Once you repent, never allow someone to throw it back in your face. If God says you are forgiven, then you are forgiven.

Pray this prayer:

Father, in the name of Jesus, I come to you now asking for forgiveness of my sins. I call them all out one by one Lord as you bring them back to my remembrance. (Begin to renounce every sin and as God reveals them, confess them to the Lord. Yes, He knows all things. But confession is also good for you.) Continue to pray: *Lord, I release all of the pain, the anger, and bitterness. I release it all Lord. I want to be happy. I want to be free and most importantly, I want to please you with my life. Change my life Lord. I release* (Begin to release all the people you need to forgive, including yourself.) *and I forgive them* (and yourself) *for all the things they did.* (Begin to name the things they did to you as a part of your cleansing process. It is okay to journal them, but there is power in spoken word. Therefore, I prefer you say this aloud as God reveals the faces, names, and incidents.) *God, I release it all unto you. Your Word says that you are the burden bearer and that I don't have to carry this weight. I release the weight of heaviness now in Jesus' name. I release all un-forgiveness in Jesus' name. Fill my heart with your love, joy and your peace, Lord. Teach me how to love again. Teach me how to trust again. Teach me how to love myself, Lord. In Jesus' name. Reveal my purpose unto me, Lord. Show me why you created me. I often feel as if I have no purpose or as if no one loves me. But God, shower down your love on me. I recognize that I need you, Lord. I no longer will try to do things on my own. But as your Word says in Matthew 6:33, "Seek ye first the Kingdom of God and all other things will be added." I love you Lord and I thank you. Here is my life Lord. Do what you may for I trust you. Help me to live a life pleasing unto you. Teach me how to overcome temptation and not give into my flesh. I love you Lord and I declare and decree that I am free in Jesus' name! I command the shackles to be loosed now in Jesus' name! I command the chains to break now in the name of Jesus!* (Flow into your heavenly language if you have one.) *I count it all done in Jesus' name. I will never look back Lord. In Jesus' name, I pray. Amen!*

CHAPTER 4: SINGLE BUT NOT ALONE (PART I)

"Embracing Your Singleness"

I noticed that when I first began to promote my book, it tended to capture the attention of singles; therefore, I promised that I would include this portion in the book. However, as you can see, *The Power in Waiting* is about more than just waiting on a mate. Its concept is geared toward empowering individuals to not grow weary while in their process of what God said (the promise) to the manifestation (fulfillment of His word). It is so easy to believe the Lord when everything is going well. But when everything seems to be going the opposite of what has been spoken over our lives that is when many of us become weary and discouraged. Be assured today that God is still in control and everything that is supposed to take place in our lives will occur in God's perfect timing.

One misconception that many of us tend to believe as singles is that we are alone. Because there is no one there in the natural, we forget all about what the Word of God says in regards to our heavenly Father never leaving nor forsaking us. I want to remind you that we serve a tangible, omnipresent, omnipotent God who can be everywhere, attending to all of His children, all at the same time. For He is the Alpha and Omega, the beginning and the end, and He is just bad like that! However, I do understand how it feels to climb into our beds at night, longing to feel the arms of someone around us, and are left alone feeling only our sheets and lacking the presence of someone rolling over saying, *"Goodnight honey"* or *"I love you."* Being a single woman, I truly can relate; however, remember this too is a part of the process.

There are a few things I want to share with you, especially if you are single. Before the Lord can send you a mate, you must learn to be content with Him first. The Word of God instructs us to love the Lord God with all of our heart, soul and mind (*Matthew 22:37*). It also instructs us to put no other gods before Him (*Exodus 20:3*). That means our desire for a mate should not have more of our focus than the Lord has. That means our spouse (or even our desire for one), our children, our careers, nor our money should come before the Lord. I, too, have struggled in the area of being single. For one, I grew up with my biological father being in and out of my life, and regarding the one man that I ever loved, we broke up and never seemed to be able to work it out. It was as if I became numb and only turned to men for the temporary pleasure they could offer me at the moment. I went through a stage where it did not matter that I was not the only woman they were seeing. It didn't even matter if they loved me or not. Matter of fact, I knew they didn't really love me, but to feel their arms around me, to hear the words, *"I love you"* seemed to soothe my aching soul. All I ever wanted was to be loved authentically. I just wanted to be loved simply for who I was, not for what I could offer or what was between my legs.

I know we are getting deep now, but I must be real with you in this section because many women and men (don't think it's only women) are settling for one-night stands, or are even in relationships with individuals whom they know they are not in love with and really possess no feelings for. As a matter of fact, they don't even meet your standards, but for now, they are a temporary fix and guess what my sister or my brother? That is called settling.

To some, it is better to have a piece of a man or a piece of a woman than to have no man or woman at all. Well, after I went through my promiscuous stages of allowing men to do whatever they wanted with me, only to have them leave me and go on to their next stop, I was left unsatisfied and empty. I can recall this one incident where I had met a guy at a club, and being immature and desperately in need of attention, I sat in his car and talked with him for hours and allowed him to convince me to lead him to where I lived. We went to my place and we ended up having sex. I must admit it was very pleasurable at the moment; he was very affectionate, which was a plus for me because most of the men I would meet only wanted to climb on top of you and didn't have too many words to say before or after. But this guy was different; he was very conversational and he actually stayed all night. Boy, did I think he was the one.

But ladies, let me tell you something. When you meet a guy and open your legs to him on the first night, there is no commitment coming out of that. Now don't get me wrong. I hear stories all the time of people saying they couldn't be in a relationship with someone and not know what they were working with. My response to that is, if that person is truly from God, and with God saying in His Word that He would give you the desires of your heart, then I don't believe there will be much disappointment in that area. Now, you may have to teach or show them how to cater to your needs specifically. But that is all a part of becoming *one* in a marriage.

My mind tends to steer back to the book (and later the movie) by Comedian Steve Harvey, *Act Like a Lady, Think Like a Man*. The reason his book was a number one bestseller and the movie was a hit is because the world is looking for ways to learn how to keep a man and how to keep a woman. So they turn to secular love experts for advice versus coming to the church. But do you know why they go to those people instead of the church? It is because our divorce rates are just as high in the church as it is in the world. There is just as much infidelity going on behind our pulpits and in our choirs, and fornication going on in our congregations. Therefore, the world really has no great examples as to how godly marriages truly are supposed to be. The world teaches us that it's okay to be married and have an *open* relationship. The world teaches us that it's okay to have multiple wives; some even try to use the Bible to back that up, which is a huge misinterpretation. The world teaches us that it's okay to have sex, have children, and then get married. But I am here to inform you that it was not the original plan of God. The Lord intended for sex to be amongst married couples only.

I once attended a conference and heard the prolific Bible teacher and author, Dr. Cindy Trimm, who was there to empower the women. She was encouraging us as singles to keep our legs closed. She said, *"When you have sex with a man who is not your husband, there is more than just temporary pleasure taking place, but an exchange is being made."* Many of us believe that if we make the man wear a condom, then that blocks out everything and the truth of the matter is it does not. When an unmarried man and an unmarried woman come together and decide to have sex, everything that is within that man is then deposited into the woman. In Juanita Bynum's book, *No More Sheets*, which I highly recommend if you are still having sex with individuals whom you are not married to, she states that women are receptors and men are projectors, meaning the man deposits and the woman receives.

You may ask, *"What am I receiving Carla?"* You are receiving everything that is within that man's spirit. If he struggles with lying, pornography, masturbation, or anger, when you sleep with him, all of that is being deposited into your spirit. And the very same happens to the man. When two people have sex, they become one; that's how I can understand why there must be an untangling of knots taking place in the spiritual realm because many of us have hopped, or are still hopping, from one bed to another in search of something we will never find, for we are seeking love and acceptance in all the wrong places. Perhaps you are no longer hopping in and out of the sheets with anyone, but you are still masturbating or still find yourself struggling in your spirit. Have you ever asked the Lord to untangle the knots? Have you ever asked the Lord to purge your spirit from every person you have ever slept with?

You may even ask if oral sex is included. Most certainly it is. Don't allow people to fool you into thinking that oral sex is not considered sex. Oral sex, fondling and all that *extra* stuff is still considered sex. And if it isn't, then if you fondle long enough, you will end up having sex. So either way, don't do it! Allow me tell you what happens when you don't allow the Lord to be your all and all. When you don't allow the Lord to fill every empty void, you continue to allow the spirit of lust to lead you. Webster's dictionary defines the word *lust* as intense or unbridled sexual desire. I wanted to clarify that because many people are confusing *lust* with *love*! I tell ladies all the time who like to talk about how in love they are, and how their 'boo thang' does this and does that for them. So I ask the question, *"Are the two of you being intimate?"* Normally, the answer is yes. I then ask them if they want to know truly how much he loves them. By this time, they are normally either giving me a blank stare or the phone line is dead silent. So I go on and share anyway. I tell them if you want to know how much that man loves you, tell him you have decided that you no longer wanted to have sex until you get married. Now, either one of two things tend to happen. Either he is going to marry you or he will eventually leave you. Now, if he really loves you like he claims he does, then he can put that loving on pause long enough to go out and buy a ring and set a wedding date.

At this point, let me add this since we are on this topic, and this clearly applies to men as well. Believe it or not, there are some men that feel they are being used for sex as well. Trust me, anything a woman is dealing with concerning a man, I'm sure a man is somewhere dealing with the same or a very similar situation. So, I definitely don't want this to sound like I am bashing my brothers because that is not the case at all.

Another thing I am noticing is a lot of people are getting married for all the wrong reasons. It is either because their tail is too hot and they can't find anything to help cool them off, and some ignorant person is speaking in their ear saying, *"Baby, it's better to marry than to burn."* Now scripture does support that; however, if you don't even know his last name, where he is from, what his goals are in life, how many children he has, what his AIDS status is (not what you heard, but having actually seen the official copy for yourself), then why are you considering marrying this man? Most importantly, if he is not saved *for real,* then why even look his way? The same applies to women. Brothers, if this woman is not good enough for you to bring home to meet your mother, then why allow her or others to talk you into getting married when you truly know you do not love her? Don't be fooled by her Coca Cola shape and how she bats her eyes. If you have to run out of the house like Joseph did when Potiphar's wife was trying to entice him, then you do what you have to do!

I'm sure everyone and their mama have seen *Coming to America*, but if not, check it out! It was tradition for the wife to be found for the prince, but Prince Hakeem changed the game on that one. Why? Because it was important for him to find his own wife in whom he loved and not one that would simply be there at his beckon call. To me, that movie was a great example of how marriages are supposed to be according to biblical standards. Prince Hakeem pursued Lisa. You didn't see Lisa chasing him down. As a matter of fact, she was dating someone else and was actually in love with him, until he decided to focus more on impressing her family with his riches than on pleasing her and loving her genuinely. Because the current boyfriend was rich, her father wanted her to marry him.

Aha! Doesn't that sound like many people today? Have you ever seen a beautiful woman with a downright ugly man, but you could tell by the way he carried himself that he had a little bit of change? Or ladies, have you ever seen a brother who had everything wrong with him but a third eye, but he pulled up in that all black, chromed out Bentley, stepped out with his gators, and you were like, *"Hmmm, that third eye ain't that bad!"*? We won't admit it, but oftentimes we are moved by material things versus remembering that we actually have to be able to wake up to this person every morning before they put on their Gucci and Prada and so forth! What I am trying to say here is get to know people for who they are, not what they have. Temporal things will fade away, health may decline, finances may become at an all-time low, then what happens? If you don't have genuine or agape love for your spouse, then when times get tough, you won't last because you will no longer have the things. But all you may have is one another and that won't satisfy you because the truth is, you don't really like the person!

There are so many things we can discuss as it relates to being single, but not alone and different things we tend to face as being single. But there is one thing that I have experienced that I want to share with you as it relates to the importance of allowing God to untie the spiritual knots so you can become free and not become a masked individual who pretends to be one thing when you are really something else. I want to go back to the spirit of lust, which again is defined as intense or unbridled sexual desire. I once wrestled with this spirit and because of it I was not only promiscuous with men, but also with women. Because of all the hurt I experienced from men, I chose to allow myself to be introduced to homosexuality by another young lady who showed interest in me. Now notice, I said *chose* because the truth is we are all presented with options in life and although bad things may happen to us, we have the power to not allow it to control us or even respond to it. I chose not to be a victim, but I speak from the viewpoint sharing the outcome of the choices I made. Yes, there were times I was mistreated, but even after all of that, I still had a choice to go hide in a corner, rocking back and forth, feeling sorry for myself. No. I chose to take action and cry out to the Lord and allow Him to transform my life so I could be here today, sharing this testimony with you.

If you recall earlier, I stated I had only been in love with one man in my life. But now that I think of it, actually it was two. Only this gentleman didn't love me the way I loved him. I was in love with him and wanted to be with him, and he loved me too, but not enough to stop running the streets. I remember during the time we talked, I would often try to change who I was to be the type of woman I knew he had around him. But the truth was he kept me around because of how I carried myself differently from the other women. I wasn't the woman he would take to the clubs, but we would dine at fine restaurants. I was the one driving his sports car, and he was buying me Coach bags

51

and shoes. Yet, it wasn't until later that although I had access to his car, his money and his body, no one really knew about me. This is funny because it didn't really register just how insignificant I was to him until I began sharing this story with you. Please don't get me wrong. He made me feel important; he came home every night, no matter how late it was. We slept in the same bed and I gave him sex when he wanted it. I did it all. But that is not even what puts the icing on the cake. Are you ready for this? Here goes! I did all of that and our relationship still had no title; we were just "kicking it."

How many of you reading this have a friend who no matter how much you ask them, "So what we doing or when are we going to make this official?" they are like, "Come on babe, we kicking it." I can recall him saying things to me like, "I don't spend time with no one like I spend with you. I don't open up to anybody like you." Believe it or not, during that time, those words were soothing to me. Those words helped me to sleep at night when he was out doing whatever and would come in at 2 or 3 a.m. Now this didn't last for a long time, maybe only about six months. But the point is that it happened.

I wonder how many women are reading this that have a man you are dealing with and no titles have been established. But you are cooking his food, washing his clothes, and spending his money, but you know he sleeps with other women from time to time. Perhaps you do have a title, but you still know he is not being faithful. What are you doing about it? Are you afraid to pack up and leave because you will no longer be able to maintain your celebrity lifestyle you try so hard to portray? It is because of things like this that I don't watch television shows like *Basketball Wives* or *Love & Hip Hop* because the women are so caught up in portraying to be something they are not. Furthermore, they aren't even wives, but some are girlfriends or ex-wives and they are just caught up on luxury statuses and they know the man is not being faithful to them. If this is you, know that your reputation for always having the finest, driving the finest and so forth is not worth your peace, neither is it worth your happiness. When I think of movies like *"Belly"* and *"Baby Boy,"* which are well-known movies in the African American culture, we see women dealing with infidelity as if they have no choice. What gets to me is the men aren't even their husbands, but they are either baby's daddies or boyfriends. When are we going to wake up and realize that the void we are seeking to fill with others and things are a place designed strategically for God? When are we going to realize that God wants to be the one to show us what real love is? The Lord loved you so much that He laid his life down and died for you so that you may have life and have it more abundantly.

If you are dating a man who is not willing to lay down his life for you, then you need to let him go! The sad part is we often know the man or woman is no good, but for one reason or another, we choose to stay. Some people choose to stay because they are afraid of starting over, and others may choose to stay because they may have multiple children and feel no one will want them because of the children. That is not true. If you are a mother who is holding your own, taking care of your children, keeping your house and paying your own bills the right way, a real man will notice and will be intrigued by your strength to not have a sugar daddy or not do unclean things for money, like many other women are doing nowadays. Because you have standards, a *real* man will notice you, but only in God's appointed time.

The last thing I want to share with you as it relates to lust is deal with that spirit because if you don't, you will find yourself going from pleasuring and desiring men to pleasuring and desiring women. I know there are many women or even men who may be reading this and saying, "I would never sleep with another woman" or "I would never sleep with another man." Be careful how you say that because most of the women I dated when I was in that lifestyle were everyday women, just like you. It would blow your mind the women who are actually entertaining homosexual activities. We tend to overlook women who are feminine and believe the only women who are struggling in this area are those who are more masculine. Where is your discernment? This sister comes in the church every Sunday broken, wanting to be delivered from homosexuality. But there is no one in the church spiritual enough that will turn down their plate and fast, or that can hear her cry during worship and come and help her get delivered. The reason why spiritual discernment is needed so heavily is because our churches have become extremely wicked and now you have to be careful of whom you share your struggle with. Because the next thing you know, the elder who you confided in about your struggle, you are now waking up in his bed and you are trying to figure out how in the world this happened.

This is the war cry I hear amongst the body of Christ today. A lot of people are struggling, but have no one to go to. I know how that feels because that used to be me. Struggling with lust had me stuck in the homosexual lifestyle for five years of my life, all while I was raising my young daughter. I had no one to really take me under their wing and help me get delivered and for a while, I was angry with the church because I was that girl who sat in the service Sunday after Sunday, bible study after bible study, with my girlfriend and no one in the church could discern that we both were about to burst hell wide open! One thing I learned was that I was supposed to experience what I experienced, and God had it strategically designed for no one to help pull me out until I had a divine experience with Him. It was because of the experiences I had with God in the privacy of my home that I have come to love Him deeply and learn just how much He loved me.

My deliverance process often took place right within the walls of my home. My deliverance consisted of me crying out to God in my closet, lying on the floor screaming and crying, begging the Lord to deliver me. I had lost all touch and desire for a man. The enemy even lied to me, often telling me that my desire for the natural would never be restored. But he is a liar for God restored it in His timing. I learned that I had to tarry with this spirit so that patience and compassion would be cultivated through me to want to go out and help others who felt trapped in homosexuality.

I can be honest today and say the reason I turned to women was because I was tired of being alone and mistreated by men. However, the truth is men could only do what I allowed them to do. We must be careful how we entertain the spirit of loneliness. We have to learn to deal with that spirit and cast it out in the name of Jesus! For the spirit of loneliness will have you writing a check that your behind can't cash! Either you will be left with a bump in your belly, a bump in your private area, or a torn up mind, not knowing whether you want a man or a woman! Listen to me now! It is better to wait on the Lord and allow Him to fill your most secret places. I am to the place in my walk with God now in which I have told him not to send my husband until I am 110% satisfied with Him only. I remember crying in my bed, wondering why no one loved me. I had only dated one man in my entire life that was faithful to me that I knew of. I can't even say he didn't cheat; let's just say he didn't get caught! I have been pregnant by men who were sexing me on a regular, but at the end of the day, they didn't really love me.

I can recall one guy I was sleeping with and I found out I was pregnant, and the first thing out of his mouth wasn't, *"It ain't mine!"* No, he immediately asked, *"So what you gon' do?"* I was like, "Negro, what?" But because I knew he didn't love me, I went to the clinic and had the procedure. Sadly, I even had to almost drag him to the clinic with me. If you are a woman who is reading this and have had an abortion by the suction method called vacuum aspiration, you can attest that it literally feels like they are sucking all of your organs out of your body through that small tube. I was in excruciating pain, but then guess what? After all of that, I had to drive an hour and a half back home because the boy didn't have any driver's license. Lord, the mess we get ourselves into!

I am reminded of another quote by Dr. Cindy Trimm, which I believe is one of her favorite quotes: *"Could things be the way they are because you are the way you are?"* Now that's an excellent question you should consider for a moment. Oftentimes in life, we want to blame everyone else for the troubles in our lives, but we are the main drivers. An anonymous author cited the famous quote, *"When life throws you lemons, make lemonade."* So I would like to say, I am making lemonade today. I have made a lot of bad choices in my life, which resulted in bad things happening to me as well as me being mistreated. But the best thing I could have ever done was forgive every person who ever hurt me; but more importantly, I had to forgive myself.

You are valuable to the Lord and He has need of you. If you are struggling in your flesh, today is your day to receive your breakthrough, for this is not a book that you read only for leisure; but this book will help break bondage off of your life and destroy the yoke from around your neck. I plead the blood of Jesus over your life right now! You will no longer struggle in your flesh, for a struggle is only present when you fight against the original plan of God for your life. If you are reading this and you are not saved and want to receive salvation, pray this prayer first:

Lord, I come to you just as I am. I come to you Lord, acknowledging that I am in desperate need of you. I repent of my sins Lord. I pray that you will forgive me, Lord. Your Word says that if I would confess my sins that you would cast them as far as the east is from the west. Your Word says that you will do new thing in my life. Lord, I need you to be that new thing. I will no longer run and hide, but God I surrender my total being unto you today. Take my life, do what you may, for I have no other options. My desire is to know you in a deeper way. I thank you for loving me, Lord. I thank you for forgiving me. I receive your love and I receive your forgiveness, Lord. I ask you now Father to wash me white as snow. Create in me a clean heart and renew a right spirit within me. I receive your forgiveness, Lord and I thank you, in Jesus' name. Amen.

If you are praying for deliverance in your mind and in your body, and to break the spirit of lust off of your life, pray this prayer. Know that many spirits are attached to the spirit of lust, so although you may not be struggling with certain ones, pray over all of them because they tend to connect one with another.

Lord, I come to you now as your child and I repent of my sins, Lord. I admit there were times when I did not do as you directed. I did not obey your Word, but I allowed my flesh to govern me Lord. Today, I ask that the spirit of lust be broken off of my life, Lord. I bind the spirit of lust, homosexuality, masturbation, and every unclean spirit that is attached to it. I command these spirits to be broken off of my life, in the name of Jesus! I speak to my body today and command it to bless the

*Lord! I command my spirit to rise up and be strengthened by the power of the Holy Spirit. I bind up the strong man that is associated with the spirit of lust. I renounce every action, every spoken word and Lord, I receive your salvation all over again today. I receive your Word and I desire more of you, Lord. Fill every void; go into the secret places of my heart Lord where no one knows I am hurting, but you Lord. Wrap me in your arms Lord; I long to be held by my natural father in which I have never experienced. I long to be held in the arms of my birth mother. I long to be loved genuinely Lord. Teach me how to love Lord. Soften my heart; tear down every barrier that will try to make me afraid to love again. I release all hurt, anger, resentment and confusion that has tried to consume my mind. I release every person that ever said anything negative to me (*At this time, call out their name(s). Release these people or person to the Lord). *Lord, I exchange fear for faith. Your Word says that faith comes by hearing, and hearing by the Word of God. So Lord give me a hunger and thirst for your Word and help me to not just be a hearer only, but also a doer of your Word. Take my life Lord and use it for your glory. Lord, I receive your love and I receive your forgiveness. Lord, I don't want just another experience, but I just want you. Show me that you are real. So many people are playing Lord and claiming one thing and living another. But I want to be authentic, Lord. I bind up the spirit of hypocrisy. No longer will I condemn others for doing the very*

59

things I once did. Place an insurmountable measure of love in my heart for your people, Lord. In Jesus' name, I pray. Amen!

This chapter was for singles only; for as single individuals, we tend to face more things and are often tempted to believe that our self-worth and value is in the connection of another human being. But the truth is your self-worth and value is found in Jesus. Draw nigh unto Him and He will draw nigh unto you (*James 4:8*).

CHAPTER 4:

SINGLE BUT NOT ALONE (PART II)

"What to Do Until Your Husband Finds You"

For Women Only

Letter Dedication: *I believe I am led by God to minister to single women during this season. As a single woman, I too have cried countless nights, wondering what was wrong with me. Relationships failing, fighting feelings of loneliness, and entertaining thoughts of: "Am I good enough?" "Is there something wrong with me?" "God, why am I not married?" I'm sure you too have wrestled with some of these same things or the Holy Spirit would not be prompting me to be transparent and share this information with you. I am here to tell you that your season of marriage will come, but even the greatest blessing can be a curse if it lacks preparation and is given prematurely.*

Scriptural Focus: _Ecclesiastes 3:1_: *"To everything there is a season and a time to every purpose under the heaven..." Discern your season ladies! For single women, this is our season to forsake all and draw closer to the Lord and being committed, faithful & loyal to HIS business. Be faithful to Him without cheating on Him by sleeping with other men, and He will bless you with the man of your dreams. Try God and see won't He not just bless you, but literally BLOW...YOUR...MIND!*

I too have run into days full of discouragement and I found myself asking, *"When God, when?"* I remember thinking, *"I am a beautiful woman. I am the publisher of an amazing magazine. I am soon to be launching two other businesses. I live in a fine home. I drive a nice car. I have a beautiful daughter. I am passionate about ministry, and am totally committed to the things of God. In my mind, any man would be blessed to have a woman like me!* How many of you will be honest and say, *"Yeah Carla, that sounds like me too."*

Well, the facts are just that ladies, just *any* man can't have a woman of your caliber. We are beautifully and wonderfully made, created with destiny in mind, and God will not allow all of His hard work to be tainted by some Bozo. We must stop allowing people to lead us to believe that we are missing something because we choose to be selective in who we date and not jump on the first thing that comes our way. We are royalty; we are children of the King! (Note: Jesus is not a king, but *the King!*) When have you ever seen king's kids accepting anything less than the best?

My sisters, I am here to share with you *The Power in Waiting*. When God gave me this title so many things came to my mind. I thought of the power in waiting for a mate, the power in waiting for the manifestation of what God said (via prophecy or directly from God), the power in waiting before having sex, the power in waiting on your turn. My mind began to flutter with many different things in which I could share with you all, but the Holy Spirit led me to share with women the power in waiting on God for their husbands and to stop trying to choose one for themselves. OUCH! Truth be told, many women find it okay to approach men nowadays in an effort of helping them if they appear to be shy or possibly suffer from rejection. One thing I learned about men is they are hunters by nature and if there is something they want badly enough, then trust me, baby boy will learn how to open his mouth and approach you. Please note that I never said what would come out of his mouth would be appropriate, but real men aren't afraid to speak up.

In sharing this, we as women must learn to relax and be anxious for nothing as the Word of God tells us and be reminded that good things come to those who wait. I know the Bible also says it is better to marry than to burn, but I would rather experience life as a single woman than to be married to the wrong man who beats me and hinders me from reaching my destiny.

I want to provide you with some vital information as it relates to waiting:

Why Waiting is Beneficial:

■ Waiting helps develop your character and prepare you for the transition of becoming a wife.

■ Waiting allows you to get to know God as not only your spiritual Father, but your mate as well, for Christ must be your *first* love.

■ Waiting produces patience, which you will need along this journey called life.

How Do I Wait?

■ Wait *in* God! Prophetess Juanita Bynum has a song called, *Don't Mind Waiting* in which she shares with us how we are no longer waiting *on* God, but we are to wait *in* Him. Allow God to share His heart with you by using this time as a single woman to give God *all* of you. Don't hold anything back. Commit to a life of prayer, fasting, and holy living. Not saying you can't have fun, but always be mindful of the settings and who you connect to.

What Do I Do While Waiting?

■ Enjoy being with Jesus; you can do what you want, when you want, and how you want. If you want to go on a week-long cruise, you are free to do so because there is no husband at home pouting because you are out hanging with your girlfriends.

■ Give yourself 1000% to ministry.

■ Hang out with your girlfriends, those who can add to your life and not subtract from it! (Assets vs. Liabilities)

■ Go back to school.

■ Start a book club.

■ Learn how to cook. *("You want to be married and your nails too long to make a biscuit"*-Prophetess Juanita Bynum- No More Sheets)

■ Learn how to keep your house clean.

■ Get into God's Word and learn more about what He desires for your life.

I have read a lot of books that helped me embrace my singleness and learned how to wait on God to bring my mate. And as I wait on God, I have learned to enjoy Him, put Him first, and allow Him to be my spiritual Husband until He sends my earthly husband. I have also listened to a lot of videos as it relates to ministering to single women. But nothing really ministered to my spirit like these books listed below. I am sharing with you every tool I have that helped me master my life as a single woman living victoriously. My prayer is that you would add these books to your library, one by one, and I guarantee they will bless you!

Kimontheweb.com - Kimberly Brooks is the author of *How to Date and Stay Saved*, which caters 100% to single individuals. Her book supplies you with how far to go while dating, the true purpose of dating, as well as answering questions that thousands of singles have. Check out her website for inspirational articles dealing with various issues as it relates to living the single life.

The Victorious State of Mind-Lakeisha Dixon (www.lakeishadixon.com) - This powerful manual will help you overcome the battle in your mind and teach you step by step how to live a victorious life. This book isn't necessarily about being single, but it helped me to think positive and forced me to change my mindset on being single in the flesh, but married to Jesus, knowing that my life was in His hands. So again, it is not written directly to singles, but it will positively impact your life and help you think the right things on purpose!

Sassy, Single & Satisfied - Author Michelle McKinney Hammond shares the secrets to enjoying everyday life as a single woman and learning to focus on what you *do* have rather than what you *don't.* She teaches us how to get our priorities in order, squeeze the most out of being single, prepare for your mate, and have your deepest desires fulfilled, which are areas that only God can fill. I have actually read this book quite a few times and it's very refreshing every single time!

No More Sheets, The Truth About Sex - Dr. Juanita Bynum: This book will help you get out of the sheets. Like me, Dr. Bynum is transparent as it relates to her experiences and struggles with being in and out of the sheets. This book changed my life and I still use it as a guide today. One of the chapters in the book that I loved the most was entitled *Masturbation.* This chapter blessed me the most because it was one of my struggles and because I allowed others to talk in my ear. I began to think that it was okay to *'take care of myself.'* I allowed the enemy to make me think that because I was not actually having sex with a person, that it was okay to do it. But the truth is I was having sex with all of my exes all over again, *in my mind!* Many singles today struggle in this area and have no resources to help them because they can't just pick up the Bible and see it clearly say, *"Don't masturbate."* However, the Bible does tell us to think on those things that are pure. It also goes on to tell us to cast down vain imaginations and anything that exalts itself against the knowledge of God. That clearly means those thoughts that come to influence that your body is in need of a *fix,* you must learn to cast down those thoughts and begin to declare what the Word of God says aloud. Now, don't get me wrong; I messed up a lot before I actually learned how to use the weapon of God's Word and the weapon of spiritual tongues to defeat the enemy.

The Bible tells us that if we resist the enemy, then he will flee. Many of us are failing these tests because we simply won't use our resistance and say no to the enemy. The Bible tells us to overcome evil with good. There was a time I was used to having sex every night and during my deliverance process, the hardest and toughest times for me were at night. I remember for over six months straight, I went to be bed listening to my sermons of my pastor preaching every single night. If it wasn't him preaching, it was worship music. Then, one night after I had been doing that for a while and I thought I no longer needed to go to bed with the sermons and the worship music playing, I fell asleep. But I remember waking up in the middle of the night and I tell you; boy, were my hormones raging. In a matter of moments, I slipped up and masturbated again! But, do you see how the enemy works? He didn't do it when I first laid down because he knew I would have jumped up and turned on the CD of my pastor preaching or the worship music. But he waited until I had a vulnerable moment, was not alert, and he crept in. I remember repenting right afterward and I felt so bad. Finally, I was reminded of what Juanita Bynum said in this book. She said, *"Whatever it took for you to get free, it will take that and some more in order for you to stay free."* So, if you find yourself struggling in this area, go get her book and no one ever has to know, for she has strategically placed the subject inside her book.

Never Give Up - Joyce Meyer: This book is not necessarily dedicated to singles either, but I added it because the Lord had me to specifically focus on getting free from the spirit of lust. I know that when you desire to be free, it doesn't always take place in one setting or instance. If you are like me, my deliverance took place over a period of time. This book will encourage you to never give up. No matter how much I messed up, I would always hear the words, *"Never give up!"* and it would empower me to dust myself off and try it again. Eventually, after a lot of bumps and bruises, I stand here today, delivered, whole and set free from Satan's grip from the various things he tried to use to destroy me. The same can happen for you now if you receive God's love now!

Lady in Waiting: Becoming God's Best While Waiting for Mr. Right by Jackie Kendall & Debby Jones: This book blessed me ladies, especially when it talked about how we must be women of reckless abandonment, meaning we must forsake all to follow the Lord and know that our ultimate fulfillment comes from Him and not in another human being. This book also taught me that until I connected with God and allowed Him to fill every void that was intended for Him from the beginning, then a man would never be able to love me to satisfaction, for I would always be in search of what was meant for God the whole time. Lastly, this book taught me how to tear up my list and *become* the list. So often, we as women (and men) can have such grand expectations, such as he must be this tall, drive this kind of car; or guys, she has to have pretty feet and no kids. But, you have five kids yourself and your feet look like they belong on a gorilla. This is comical, but it is true. You too ladies; you say you want a man that makes six figures, or must be light skinned with curly hair, when you don't even make six figures and you busy wearing weave down your back talking about, *"I got Indian in my family."* Please stop it! *Lady in Waiting* really changed my life and it helped me focus more on me and work on my relationship with God more than my future spouse. It directed me to center my attention on things that are more important in a spouse, such as his relationship with the Lord, whether he is family-oriented, and whether he respects his mama. These are things we should take notice of before we are moved by his Mercedes Benz or how bowlegged he is! Yes, I went there! Ya'll are not fooling me! I may be young, but I started early and I have been there, done that!

Please understand, I know we are physical beings; however, there has to be balance. At one time, all I dated was preachers and sadly, many of them I couldn't stand after we left the church! Now, I loved them in the pulpit and loved how God used them, how the people responded to them and how well respected they were. But, once we got back home or busy in our day-to-day lives, they weren't gentlemen, were not faithful, and were not into being abstinent. So, I tell you my sisters; don't be moved by what you see on the outside. Develop some discernment and allow God to show you that man's heart, his soul, his intellect, and his inner most desires that he won't share

69

with you at first or maybe ever. So many women want to be married so badly that they are settling for men that are beating on them and cheating with other women, which they know about! Rise up today my sisters if this is you! Know that you don't have to be desperate and that you are worth the wait. All of this, *"What you won't do, another woman will"* mess--stop it! If your man or a man ever says that to you, *run!* Never allow your emotions, or because you *love* him, to cause you to compromise when God has clearly declared that you be holy, for He is holy and requires that we present ourselves as a living sacrifice, holy and acceptable unto the Lord. So what if he walks out because you decided to close your legs; take a praise break and shout right there, for the Lord just spared your life! Trust and believe that if your man can't wait until you say, *"I do"* to marry you, then become a *Lady in Waiting* and know that in spite of what statistics prove, all of the good brothers are not taken, gay, or in jail. But there are some good brothers out there. You must believe that if God hasn't sent him yet, then He is still working on some things within you, as well as within him. So, know there is truly *Power in Waiting.*

CHAPTER 5:

DON'T LET YOUR MIND TALK YOU OUT OF IT

Have you ever felt the urge to step out and do something unorthodox or unusual, such as invest in a particular stock, open a business, or plan a vacation to Europe? Although it may not have been one of those things, the point I am making is I'm sure all of us can relate to times when the Lord showed us a vision about something and instead of us getting excited about it and writing down all He begins to share with us, we begin to worry and think about the *who, what, when and where.* We literally allow our minds to provoke us to worry when clearly our Bible tells us that God is not only one who gives us vision, but He also makes provision. God will never show us something and then not supply us with what we need to bring it to pass. So often, we can simply think too much and allow our mind to talk us right out of the very thing the Lord was directing us to do.

I will use myself for example. On September 7, 2012, I hosted my first women's conference in my hometown and the truth is the Lord had given me that vision earlier in the year around the month of February. Here I was, this 28-year-old young minister who had no experience on how to conduct a conference. When the Lord first gave it to me, my mind immediately went into overload and I began to think, *"But Lord, who will come? What if I plan this event and no one shows up? But Lord, I have no clue what I am doing. Who is going to help me?"* I also began to think, *"What are people going to say? What are they going to think?"*

You have to understand this is the very same city in which I had grew up in and ran around town with my girlfriends, partied, drank and did everything I wanted to do. Then, within only a short time in ministry, the Lord chooses me to host a conference in my hometown? I tell you, I was excited and afraid at the same time. One thing I have learned about fear is it will rob you of your peace. Fear will cause you to focus on things that don't even matter or exist. Fear will cause you to be afraid of what *may* happen or *what if* this or *what if* that. Again, I repeat, don't let your mind talk you out of it! I remember praying and saying, *"Ok Lord, I have no clue what I am doing, but I am going to trust you to connect me with the right people and show me how to do this."* One thing my mentor/coach, Nanette Floyd Patterson always told me, *"You are the way you are for a reason. The reason why you look, act and talk the way you do is all according to God's purpose for your life."* I remember her telling me that as we talked outside after a church service one day. So I began to think about the organizational skills, and my ability to delegate and do things in excellence. I began to tap into my spiritual power and began to fast and pray, asking the Lord to lead and guide me. The more I did this, the more things began to flow. Don't get me wrong; there was a lot that I learned from conducting this conference that I will do differently for my conference next year. But the point I am making is all that I needed to complete this task was already within me, but fear and negative thoughts were trying to deter me away from what God was instructing me to do.

So I ask you, what is it that God has been tugging at you to do, but you haven't moved yet because you are waiting on the finances or you are waiting on the building or something else? Do you not know that once we step out on faith, the Lord is faithful to perform His Word? A lot of times, money is not what we need, for the money is already there. We just need to learn the strategy on how to get the money. Even today as it relates to my magazine, *Women of Standard,* my prayer is more geared not so much on things, but that the Lord will reveal the strategy to me on how to get what is right within my reach. See, one thing about God is that He plays fair. He won't bless your neighbor with a Bentley and leave you still having to catch the bus to go to work. Well, first of all, if you are neighbors with someone who has a Bentley and you have to catch the city bus to work, either their priorities are mixed up or you are actually in a great place. I have noticed many people today will live in a torn down home, but will be driving a Mercedes or BMW, and in my mind, I am like, "Huh?"

I remember I dated a guy that had a very nice car, but when I visited him in his home, it was like he was literally living as a poor person. Now, what was wrong with that picture? Habitually, we do things trying to impress people and cause them to like us when really, we need to be focused on God and fulfilling His purpose for our lives. A lot of people are stuck because they are so busy watching others and seeing how God is blessing them instead of positioning themselves to be blessed. Choose today not to allow your mind or others to talk you out of what the Lord has told you to do. Position yourself to be the best you that you can be!

One decision I made a long time ago was to never allow anyone, not even myself, to stand in the way of my destiny. Sometimes, you have to pray that the Lord delivers you from *you!* It's not always other people that hinder us, but sometimes we get in our own way! This is what I like to call the enemy vs. the *inner me.* Say this aloud: *"I will no longer stand in my own way. But I will get out of the way so God can come in and do as He may as it relates to my life."* We get in our own way by allowing others to remind us of our past, not forgiving those who have hurt us, not forgiving ourselves, or even holding our own past over our heads. My question to you today is when are you going to let it go? You must know today that your past has a purpose and although you may have made many mistakes, those mistakes are worth more than all the things you did right. Confused, huh? Let me help you.

It is because of my struggle with homosexuality, masturbation, being promiscuous, getting pregnant at a young age, being rejected, and all of those other things that caused me to write this book you are reading today. It is because of me struggling and not knowing my real identity in God that He prompted me to begin a newsletter (which today has transitioned into a blazing magazine) entitled *Women of Standard.* One thing about God, He doesn't see us as we are right now, in our present state, but He sees us as the finished product. The first time I heard God call me a woman of standard, I cried like somebody had died. I could not accept Him calling me that and for the longest time, I rejected it because *in my mind,* I remembered the things I had done and how I was still struggling in my flesh. But one precious thing I learned about God is He never changes

His mind toward us. He chose us before the foundation of the world, so there is absolutely nothing that can make Him give up on us or cause Him to love us less. Actually, believe it or not, there is nothing you can even do to cause God to love you more than He already loves you.

So, how can you begin getting out of your own way? First, begin to obey the voice of the Lord. Wherever you are right now, pause and give God a surrendered, "Yes." Gospel Artist William McDowell has a song that says, *"My life is not my own, to you I belong, I give myself away."* You must choose to give yourself completely over unto the Lord. He didn't create us to do what we wanted to do, but He strategically placed us here. How long are you going to waste time and not do what the Lord has called you to do? You have a purpose, God has a plan, and He wants to reveal it to you if only you would sit still long enough for Him to talk with you. For some of you reading this, God has already given you clear instructions and you either are allowing the opinions of others or your own personal opinions of yourself to hinder you, or you are still stuck in your past.

Ladies, do you not know there is a *pearl* within you? My coaching program is entitled *Defining the Pearl in You*. Within this program, I teach women how to love the *real* them. As women, we tend to wear so many masks so I walk them through a process of unveiling the real them and unmasking themselves. I teach them to not be afraid to say, *"I'm hurt"* or *"I'm wounded."* My focus is on instructing women how to embrace their uniqueness and be authentic. I also teach them that they must love every part of them from the mistakes they made to the great things they have done, for it all has helped shape them into who they are today. Honestly, after all the mistakes I have made, if I had the opportunity to do it all over again, I wouldn't change a thing. I used to say I would change getting pregnant and having to raise my daughter as a single mother and her father living in a separate home. But my daughter has been one of the greatest blessings of my life and it is because of all I have gone through as a single mother and woman that I am able to pour into you on today. Never regret where you come from or what your past may consist of. One thing about God is He can change your name and He can change your story. If He can transform Saul, who was once a killer of Christians, into Paul, one of the greatest and most influential apostles in the Bible, then surely He can do it for you! I also share with women the importance of knowing who they are and whose they are, and never settling for anything less than God's best. I am a firm believer that when you know who you are, you fight this fight of faith differently. The Bible says we are more than conquerors through him that loved us (*Romans 8:37*).

Speaking of the Bible, we must grow to a place that we choose to take God at His Word, stop doubting and thinking too much. Remember the title of this chapter is *Don't let your mind talk you out of it.* Stop trying to grasp all of God in your natural mind; it is not humanly possible. God is bigger than anything you could ever think of or imagine. The things God wants to do in your life are way bigger than you can even fathom. Your thoughts are too small, and He wants you to come up higher and rise up and be the man or woman He has created you to be. It is time that we know our worth and stop comparing ourselves to others. But then again, we must learn how to develop our own uniqueness and be confident in who we are.

I was always very insecure about having a long torso and not having a big behind. I know your mouth just dropped to the floor, but I believe the only way in helping others is to be real about your struggles and obstacles, for this is how we overcome. Trust me, whatever you are dealing with, there are hundreds of people dealing with the same thing; therefore, your voice is vital because they will gain hope once they hear your testimony of what the Lord has done in your life. That is what this book is all about-- sharing my struggles, failures and successes to show you that if God can deliver me out of my issue(s), and oh how I had many, then surely He can deliver you! He is no respecter of persons. But what matters most is not what others say, but what you say to yourself and what you speak over your own life. You must learn to not allow your mind to talk you out of what the Lord said you can have. Don't let your mind give you a thousand reasons as to why you can't have what God said is already yours.

Due to my insecurity about not having a big butt, I would wear butt pads. See, I am just telling it all, huh? By the time you finish reading my book, you are going to know all of my business. But that's ok, whatever it takes to help you get from where you are to where God desires you to be.

Now, there was a time when I hated the color of my eyes; I felt they were too dark and I would always wear pure hazel-colored contacts. One day, I said, "*You know what? It is what it is! If a man wants me, he will just have to be happy with what I have because the Lord didn't give me a big butt!"* I have some hips on me now, but my behind just didn't have any weight on it, as female comedian Sommore said in the *Queens of Comedy*. I literally laughed inside as I typed this because I was so trapped in trying to be what I felt others wanted me to be. I always thought I had a big nose, and I already had big puffy eyes. I'm telling you, no matter how much sleep I got, my eyes were always puffy. After a while, I said, *"Maybe this is just how my eyes are!"* So to fix that, I wore contacts in which I became so accustomed to that I was sleeping in them. I wore them improperly because I hated how I looked without them. One day, my doctor took me off of them and told me that not enough oxygen was getting to my eyes and that I had to wear the clear contacts for a few months. Her telling me that was like telling me someone in my family had just died. I know you may be laughing, but I guarantee some of you women reading this, if the stores stopped selling weaves and makeup, you would go crazy for a moment, too! I literally broke down crying in the doctor's office and I began to have a pity party and begged the doctor not to do that to me. I told her how ugly I thought I looked without my contacts and she began to sympathize with me and showed me the damage it was doing to my eyes. Then she mentioned glasses and that made me cry even more because I had worn glasses all my life and I totally hated them! Although I had nice glasses, I hated having to wipe them off whenever I would get caught in the rain, or in the mornings if the weather was foggy or humid, my glasses would fog up and I just hated it! I was forced to wear my natural eye color contacts for a few months and I noticed that my confidence level went down. I felt and believed that guys no longer looked at me or thought I was attractive. Finally one day, I began to tell myself that I am beautiful and wonderfully made and that my contacts didn't define me. I believe I talked to myself in the mirror almost every day before leaving home, which was perfectly fine. You do what you have to do to get your confidence level up.

People ask me if I am against cosmetic or plastic surgery and my response always surprises people. I tell them cosmetic surgery has its pros and its cons. I have witnessed plastic surgery used in a positive manner due to people who have been in car accidents and their faces were left disfigured; therefore, plastic surgery helped put them back together again. However, with cosmetic surgery, I believe some women just go too far. I do understand if you want to have a tummy tuck or breast augmentation because honestly, if I had the money I would probably do it, too. We always want to judge others for what they do, but the truth is if we had the money we would enhance how we look as well. However, no matter how much I hated my nose, I could never consent to having anyone perform any type of surgery on my face unless it was medically necessary. I was always afraid that they may make my nose too small and then my head was already big so I would really look weird. Now bold people like Atlanta Housewives, NeNe Leakes, had her nose done and it looks fabulous! But Michael Jackson on the other hand, God rest His soul…ok, you get my point. Basically what I am saying is I don't believe there is anything wrong with enhancing how you look; just don't lose the *real* you underneath all of the makeup, fake hair, and so forth. Many women, if they took their makeup, wigs, and undergarments off, they would literally have all of us running around screaming! Now regarding the butt pads, I no longer wear them. Instead, I have learned to buy clothing that compliments my figure. I notice that low-rise jeans look better on me than regular jeans, and jeans with pockets look better on me than jeans without pockets. Real quick, let me say this: Some of us ladies are going way too far with the eyelashes. I honestly thought they were intended for a natural look to maybe extend what you currently have; but the women I have come across have looked so unnatural and the lashes were so thick that it looked like they struggled to keep their eyes open. Now I understand for major hair shows that is necessary; but for everyday wear, such as going to Wal-Mart or the movies, you may want to rethink that. I know this is comical, but true. You ladies with lashes, don't be getting mad at me now; I'm just saying let's have balance in all we do. You know some of us can simply go overboard with the cosmetic surgery, makeup, and hair. My question to you is what are we really trying to cover up when we pack on makeup and go above and beyond with our hair? A lot of times as women, we tend to focus more on dressing up the outside (focusing on our outer appearance) because we are hurting or don't really like who we are and what we see when we look in the mirror. But we must learn to love that person that stares back at us because at the end of the day, that is all we have to work with. I believe we must learn to love ourselves from the inside out. No matter what you decide in relation to how you carry yourself ladies, do what makes you happy. But don't compromise losing the *real* you in the process.

CHAPTER 6:

ARE YOU REALLY READY

FOR THE PROMISE?

My hopes are that by now, you understand my goal in writing this book is more about you rather than what you are waiting on God for. When we find ourselves between prophesy and manifestation, I believe the *waiting time* we often experience is due to God wanting to prepare us for what is to come. You know, I like to use myself as an example. I have always wanted to be married, even when I dated women. I always knew I would never marry a woman for I always told myself that I was only doing it until the right man came along. Well, the truth is a good man who really wanted to love me and be with me did enter into my life, but I chose a woman over him. So often we think we are ready for what we currently desire, but the truth is if God really blessed us with all we longed for before proper preparation, our lives would end up in a disaster. Imagine God giving you all that you asked for at this moment in your life. Would you really be able to handle it? Some people are even praying for God to bless them with a million dollars when they don't even faithfully tithe off of the thousand dollars they are earning now. If that's you, just do like we do in church, say, "Ouch," repent and get it right. On this journey, even as a young woman, I learned that the very things I really thought I was ready for I wasn't quite ready for it at all. There were several areas of my life I could mention, but there is one area in particular that stands out to me, and that is the area of relationships.

After enduring the process of being delivered from homosexuality, failing tests and passing tests, and then failing again and back to passing again, I finally gained deliverance. Now, how I knew I was delivered was because my appetite was no longer the same. I no longer viewed women as I once did before. My heart no longer longed for a tender touch by a woman or to be intimate with a woman. But my heart began to be filled with more of pleasing God and being with Him. However, as a human being in a natural body, I slowly began to desire men again because during my unnatural experiences, I had lost all attraction, touch, smell, and affection toward men. I remember trying to be intimate with a man during my process, thinking that would help take away my desire for women, and my body just would not respond at all. If you are a woman or man who is struggling in the area of homosexuality, let me help you by saying that hooking up with the opposite sex will not decrease the desire you have. However, it may suppress it temporarily; but trust me, it will flare up again. The only thing that can take that desire away is God and undergoing His process and His way.

So, after not being with women for a while, I thought I was ready to be with men again. Thus, I began dating this guy and nothing he did satisfied me; from the way he held me, touched me, kissed me, or even talked to me. To me, it seemed all too rough. Yes, I made the same mistake that many others have who wrestled with this spirit make; I began sleeping with the guy, which only made matters worse because I later learned that I was neither free from all the women I had been with nor the men even prior to that. Therefore, when I was intimate with my current boyfriend, he was being attacked by all of the spirits that were on the inside of me, left behind from men and women I had dated. What had developed was nothing but soul ties.

Well, you may ask, *"Exactly what are soul ties?"* I honestly can't find it anywhere in the Bible where it literally uses the words *soul ties,* but it does say in Ephesians 5:31, *"For this cause shall a man leave his father and mother and shall be joined unto his wife, and they shall be one flesh."* According to this scripture, we learn the connecting of souls was created by a husband and wife. I honestly believe that is why we thoroughly enjoy intimacy. It is how God designed it, but it was for married couples only. I believe this to be true because once you have sex with another individual, in the spirit realm you actually become *one* with that person. I once attended a conference where Dr. Cindy Trimm ministered and she informed the ladies there that *sex was more than about the physical, but it was a spiritual thing.* I agree with what she said because after carefully examining my own life, I noticed I honestly have only really loved one man and that is my daughter's father. I have loved no other man like I have loved him. Now many others I *thought* I loved due to the emotional attachment I felt after having sex with them, whether it was one time or several times.

Think about it. You ever have sex with someone once, and yet they still manage to cross your mind every so often? Now, this is whether it was a pleasurable experience or not. If you would be honest, you would have to admit that the individual crossed your mind after the two of you were intimate and departed. This is because of the connection that took place in the spirit. Therefore, every time unmarried people have sex, they actually become married to that individual in the spirit. Scary, isn't it?

See, the Bible tells us we perish for the lack of knowledge. So all this talk about 'what I don't know won't hurt me' is a bunch of malarkey and we should choose our words more wisely. This is why I encourage women who are married not to just lay dormant and allow their husbands to roam the streets and sleep with different women, and then come back home to become intimate with them. What is really happening is he is bringing home the spirits he is fighting and whatever spirits the women are fighting that he's sleeping with. Now, I am not saying divorce him, for I believe that is a decision that an individual would have to make on their own. But you do have the right to protect yourself or as my pastor mentioned in our singles seminar, even if you have to make your husband wear condoms until he is tested, do it. We do have the right to protect ourselves. I tell my daughter all the time, you only get one body and one mind and it's up to you how you take care of it! That's why in the last chapter, I emphasized not to allow your mind to talk you out of it; being whatever it is God has told you that you can do, but you can't believe it at the moment that God will and can bring it to pass.

Believe it or not, whatever you feed your mind with is what will talk back to you! Think about it. If you feed your mind the Word of God, when a trial appears or temptation arises, what will pop back up in your mind? The Word! Now if you sit around and watch nothing but

Basketball Wives and fill your mind with a bunch of negativity, that is what will consume your mind.

In this chapter, my question to you is, *"Are you really ready for the promise?"* If you are a woman and desire a husband, are you really ready for him to show up in your life right now? If he showed up right now, would he find your credit tore up, your house nasty, you in debt up to your neck and your kids running all over the place? Or would he find your heart settled, you being content, you handling your home well, and if you do have children, they are very well mannered, your house is clean, you know how to cook, and your finances are under control and you are not seeking a man to save you? A lot of women don't really want a husband; they desire a sugar daddy. I had a conversation with a lady one time and she began to tell me how the man of her dreams had to drive a certain type of car and be a millionaire and so forth. Well, now that God has processed me and cleansed my mind and I am steady working on increasing and improving my relationship with Him on a daily basis, I tend to view things a little differently. So, I began to look at her and think (I didn't say this aloud), *"You aren't even driving a nice car, and as a matter of fact, you don't even have a car. Every time I turn around your response is, "It's in the shop." You yourself barely have enough income to carry you from week to week, but you want your husband to be a millionaire?"*

Many of us have false expectations as it relates to a mate and this is why we always end up heartbroken and experiencing one failed relationship after another. I believe the reason for this is because we have not allowed God to

86

fill our spirits and love us as He desires to love us, and allowed Him to validate us instead of seeking validation from other men. Or perhaps you are a man and you want her to be a certain height and her measurements must be 36-24-36; yet, you are overweight and one cheeseburger away from a heart attack. She has to be in top-notch shape, but your treadmill has layers of dust on one side and last week's laundry on the other side. Or you say she has to know how to submit unto you when you haven't fully submitted yourself unto the Lord. So how dare you expect a woman to submit unto you? Or perhaps you say, "*I don't want a crazy woman.*" But you are constantly doing things that make women go off on you like cheat, lie, and then make up excuses for why you did what you did. One thing I try to do is be fair because I have witnessed crazy things on both sides as it relates to men as well as women. I have dated men who say things like, "All women are crazy," and I have also heard women say, "All men are dogs." But I truly beg to differ, for if more women would stop allowing these men to get away with the cheating, the lying, and so forth, then men wouldn't do half of what they do. Also, men should learn how to be honest and tell a woman that you are not interested in taking things any further instead of sleeping with her, then trying to tell her that you are married or that you no longer want to see her. The point I am trying to convey here is whatever you are seeking God for, you have to begin to make room for it to show up in your life.

As a single woman, I desire a man of God whom I can do ministry with, who loves God, who is one of faith, integrity, skilled in the business arena, walks in honesty, is anointed, family-oriented and most of all, will love me as Christ loved the church as well as love my daughter as his own. Now don't get it twisted, I also desire for him to be attractive in *my* eyes. He may not look like Morris Chestnut or Shemar Moore to *you,* but as long as he is gorgeous in *my* eyes, that's all that matters! It is important to me that I am attracted to my man because I am a very affectionate individual and it's hard to be affectionate with someone you are not attracted to. So, ladies don't get caught up in loving how hard that he preaches that you forget that you have to look at that grizzly bear when you wake up in the morning! Men, don't forget that in spite of how big her behind is when she turns around, she might look like Sha-Nay-Nay (from the hit television show *Martin)*, then you are the one who has to look at her.

My life now is totally surrendered unto the things of the Lord. I relocated to a new church; I have a new pastor and First Lady; I released my first book and recently celebrated one year (October 2012) since the establishment of my magazine. God is indeed doing many new things in my life. Although I desire to be married and intend to only do it once, I do not allow thoughts of marriage to consume my mind. If I think about it too much, I find myself becoming anxious, and the Bible instructs us not to be anxious for anything, but by all things with prayer and supplication (*Philippians 4:6*). So, I encourage you to make room for whatever you would like to see added in your life. If it is as simple as creating a new wardrobe, then give some of your old clothes and shoes away to make room for the new things that are to come. If you are believing God to bless you and your spouse with your first child, trust God and begin selecting baby names and praying for your child that has yet to be conceived. Single ladies, pray for your husband; single men, pray for your wives, for in God's appointed time, your paths will cross and I'm sure they will have been well worth the wait. How are you currently preparing for the promises that God has for you? Are you speaking life over your situation daily? Are you finding scriptures to compliment what you believe God for? Whether it is a promotion on your job or believing God for a loved one to receive salvation, never stop believing and prepare for what you want to see manifested in your life.

I am in such a peaceful place right now. I remember crying almost every night from not having a man in my life to love me, show concern, or to simply ask me how my day was. I would focus on what I didn't have versus all the many blessings the Lord had bestowed upon me. My father not being in my life truly caused a void in my life, but I can't allow that, even as a grown woman, to cause me to be so desperate for love that I embrace the first man that shows me any attention or that asks me on a date. That's another thing single ladies. Stop accepting every invitation that comes your way. I received a dinner invitation from a guy that I used to be intimate with, even though we had refrained from speaking to one another. Now, this goes back to filling your thoughts with the Word of God because when he invited me, my spiritual alarm went off immediately saying, "DON'T GO BACK!" He was a man that I really cared for, but he didn't want to commit and I literally waited on him, not too long, but long enough. Since he had the problem of choosing to give up the bachelor's life, and uniting with me in a monogamous relationship, I left him and the friendship. Funny that I say I left him because he never belonged to me. I heard someone say in the movie *The Preacher's Kid, "Strays don't belong to no one."* That was an eye opener for me because I was literally being intimate with him, knowing he was intimate with other women. One thing I can never understand about men is how they can sleep with all the women they want, but when women do it...Whoooo! They get called all types of names. I tell you, I thank Jesus so much for deliverance because I had one word for myself: *a hot mess!* But, I chose not to be the woman I once was before. It all starts with a choice; one decision.

Dr. Cindy Trimm poses the question during her speaking events, *"Could things be the way they are because you are the way you are?"* Could you still be single simply because you are not yet ready for marriage? Could you still be making the money you are making because you are afraid to apply for that job out of fear of not being chosen or rejected as the candidate? Is your family torn apart because you choose not to bridle your tongue, to stop gossiping, and repeating everything that is said? Many are seeking what they should actually be doing in the meantime while they find themselves between the promise and the physical manifestation of what God has already said He would do. The reason I specified *physical* is because all that God has promised has already been done in Heaven; we are only waiting for the manifestation to take place on the earth. I love how the Bible says, *"Better is the end of a thing than its beginning"* **(Ecclesiastes 7:8).** It doesn't matter how I start out, but it's how I finish.

When I was broken, God saw me whole; even when I was in my mess, He saw me delivered. That is why He was able to call me a woman of standard while I was still in search of my identity. God used His prophets to speak over my life to confirm what He had already shown me to prove to me that I was really hearing from Him. Many of you hear from God very clearly, but you question if God is really speaking to *you.* Within your spirit, you know without a shadow of doubt the voice you are hearing is from the Lord but out of fear, and because you may not have a title, or because of your past, you feel God can't speak directly to you. Well, I am here to declare the devil is a liar! All the Lord asks is for us to be available unto Him and willing to sacrifice our lives; to live one of total obedience and submission unto Him. Establish within your servant hood that it costs to walk with Jesus because it is within Him where you obtain the fullness of joy and your peace. It is within Him where you are made whole and every wound is healed and every crooked way made straight. Therefore, I ask you again, are you really ready for the promise? If you say yes, be careful; it may cost you to give up all you have to receive the greatness as well as the fullness of all God has in store for you! So be careful of what you ask for; you just might get it!

CHAPTER 7: A DATE WITH DESTINY

The main thing I want you to walk away with after reading this book is the understanding that all you have had to endure in life, whether it was due to the actions of someone else or even things you may have brought upon yourself were only to prepare you for your date with destiny.

I don't mention the word *date* as it relates to a one time affair. However, my reference to having a date with destiny is in relation to a permanent dwelling place; meaning an appointed time.

Webster's Dictionary defines the word *destiny* as: (1) *something to which a person or thing is destined (2) a predetermined course of events often held to be an irresistible power or agency.* My interpretation is that your destiny is an ultimate arrival or place you were determined to end up at, no matter what took place prior.

I also believe the true meaning of destiny is becoming more like Jesus. Our overall purpose is to become like Him. Along this journey called life, we not only are called to reign with Christ but we also have to suffer as He suffered. Whether it is suffering in our flesh (choosing holy/righteous living over unholy/unrighteous living), or suffering persecution for standing up for what we believe in by simply echoing what God says in His word.

But through it all, the good news is God is so patient with us therefore He doesn't cancel His plan for our lives when we mess up. For in order to become more like Jesus, I believe He allows trials and tribulations to help shape and mold us and we learn how to properly respond to things by developing a personal relationship with Him.

As I look back over my own life, over the abuse, neglect, rejection, various failed relationships, being a single mother, struggling with my identity; all of that was to prepare me for my date with destiny. I am a firm believer that one day, at God's appointed time, purpose shall meet destiny and they will collide and God's glory will fall like never before. There is nothing you can do to miss your destiny; there is nothing you can say to alter it, for just like death, we all have an exact time and date in which our natural life will end and nothing, not even our faith in God, can keep us on this earth for the rest of our lives. But the Word of God says to be absent from the body is to be present with the Lord (2 Corinthians 5:8), so that is actually great news!

When purpose meets destiny in life, then it all begins to make sense. As the Lord initiates the establishment of divine relationships, you then understand why you had to go through what you went through. That it was only to prepare you for the people who have been assigned to your life to minister to, the lives you had to save! When you approach life with that kind of mindset, subsequently you learn to appreciate the individuals who ran your name through the mud. You are able to appreciate those who said you would never amount to anything. You then appreciate those who pushed you aside and said God couldn't use you because you didn't look a certain way or because you didn't sing like Sister so and so, or could preach like Brother so and so. But I am here to remind you as we bring this book to an end that "Yes! God can use even you!" I want you to dig deep and begin to search yourself and ask, *"What do I have to offer the world?"* God doesn't have you here for you, but He still has you here for someone else! We must rid ourselves of the mentality that it is all about us for it is all about Jesus and the souls we can draw unto Him!

I am one who truly desires to please the Lord with my life and have my Heavenly Father proud of me. Many of us think we have all the time in the world when the truth of the matter is, time is running out as we speak. We must be committed to making every second, every minute, and every hour count. You have no more time to waste. What are you waiting for? Get moving!

There are individuals that are waiting for you to break free from the chains that are mentally and spiritually holding you hostage and bound. It is time for you to begin to come into the full knowledge of who you really are in God and know that He loves you and has a great plan for your life!

As you read this book, I would love to hear from you and learn how sharing my story and the wisdom the lord has given me may have changed your life, shifted your mindset and/or removed the scales from your eyes. I literally wrote only as the Holy Spirit prompted. Honestly speaking, I set deadline after deadline and missed all of them because some things I had to literally walk out and experience before I could begin writing this book.

I, too, was also tempted to not even finish the book, but I remember hearing the Holy Spirit tell me that souls would be saved and lives would be changed and their purpose would be revealed from the pages of this book.

I can remember meeting Pastor Sherry Ezzell (Groundbreakers Ministries/Kinston, NC) speaking over my life at an event I attended. She told me that as I wrote, the Holy Spirit was going to speak to me and lives would literally be transformed from the words within the pages. Now, I never told this lady I was writing a book, had never met her in my life, neither did I give her any clues on what to pray for. I literally walked up to her and said, *"God told me you have something I need. Will you pray for me?"* Without hesitation, this woman of God touched me and I could literally feel the power of God all over me. Even as I typed this, a chill went through my entire body because I remember the day so clearly and I believe the shift began then, maybe even prior. But it was something powerful about meeting her and the words she spoke over my life. I am sharing this with you to encourage you to never be afraid to reach out to individuals in who you feel the Lord is leading you to connect with!

I will never forget all the emails and Facebook messages I received from women saying, *"I don't know why, but I was praying to the Lord about this situation and He led me to your profile or your website."* I promise you, each and every time those women and even some young men were battling something that God had either already delivered me out of, or I too was currently dealing with the very same issues they were currently facing. It is never about you, but always about others.

Although I have found myself needing encouragement during situations like these, many times God will send others to me to uplift them. While in the midst of my pain and discomfort, I will be led to minister to them as the Holy Spirit would flow through me. While ministering to them, I was also ministering to myself. When I would either hang up the phone with them or reply back to their messages, I could literally feel the weights of heaviness or whatever I was dealing with be lifted off of me simply because I forgot about myself and chose to focus on the need of someone else.

Another thing I have learned is the importance of being transparent. Not only was I transparent in this book, but I am transparent via messages I preach, videos I record and also during my coaching program. Whenever and whatever the Lord leads me to share, I do so without hesitation because many people are tired of the fake and the phony and they are ready for the real deal! The real deal is not only me, but you too! Someone who won't be ashamed of where they have been or what they have been. It is because you understand you have been redeemed and the hand of God is present upon your life and enabling you to use the very thing that the enemy meant for your bad to turn it around and work it for good in your life! This goes back to understanding that what you face and go through is not for you, but for those in which God will place in your life to help.

So today I ask you: What are you doing to prepare for your date with destiny? Are you educating yourself on the skill God has given you to further advance your knowledge? Are you taking time to dig into the Word of God and study (not just read) His Word to learn what He has to say directly to you? If you are single but desire a mate, are you preparing for his arrival? Gospel singer and actress Tamela Mann has a song entitled, *"Take Me to the King,"* but how many are actually prepared to enter into the presence of the King? Once again and right now on today, I want you to choose not to waste any more time and understand that although we may find ourselves in a waiting period, that does not mean sit and do nothing. But we are to pursue God and learn His purpose and plan for our lives, surrender our own will for the will of our Father; to seek Him daily for instructions on how to carry out the day in which He has given to us. Again my sisters and brothers, be encouraged and understand there is ***POWER IN WAITING!***

ABOUT THE AUTHOR

Carla Cannon is an ordained Minister, HIScoach (Spirit-led Christian Coach), Author and Publisher of Women of Standard and Men of Standard Magazine. Her primary goal is to use her story to positively impact the lives of men and women all around the world. Her mission is to empower a hurting nation and encourage them that God can use them no matter where they are and where they have been. Through her many trials and tribulations, Carla uses her testimony to empower women through her blog, magazine and her new coaching program entitled: *Defining the Pearl in You*. Within this program, Carla teaches women all across the world how to operate in their true identity of who God has created them to be, by first learning and coming into the knowledge of who He is.

"I am a firm believer that before we can operate in the fullness of who we are and were created to be, we must first learn who God is by spending time with Him consistently"- Carla Cannon

Carla believes her purpose to be helping women overcome and turn their pain into power.

"In everything I do, I position people to gravitate closer to God and not closer to me. I can only help them by telling them about a man named Jesus but they must go to Him for themselves"- Carla Cannon

Connect with Carla Cannon Facebook at: www.facebook.com/womenofstandard and on Twitter @WOSMINISTRY. Website: www.womenofstandard.org

39460148R00059

Made in the USA
Middletown, DE
16 January 2017